BAKING WITH

PRIDE

JANUSZ DOMAGALA

murdoch books
London | Sydney

BAKING WITH PRIDE

JANUSZ DOMAGALA

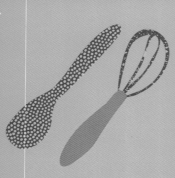

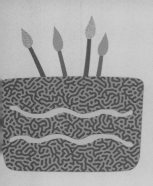

HEY HUNBUNS*

Some of you reading this might already know me, but for those of you who don't, here's the story of my journey to creating *Baking with Pride*.

My name is Janusz Domagala and I was born and raised in Sosnowiec, Poland, with my older sister, Ula, by my parents, Alicja and Jan. I'm a plus-size, body-confident, loud and proud gay baker and in 2012 I moved to Brighton, England, where I currently live with my partner, Simon, and our sausage dog, Nigel.

Although I'm a self-taught baker, I've always been adventurous in the kitchen, using recipes from Poland and the UK to create bold, weird and wonderful bakes. In 2022 my boyfriend sent off an application in secret to the TV show *The Great British Bake Off* and, as a result, I got the chance to appear on one of the most popular UK TV baking shows ever.

When I found out that I was going to be on *The Great British Bake Off*, I knew that I had an opportunity to represent a number of marginalised groups, including the LGBTQ+ community, the plus-size community and those who had to emigrate for a chance to live a safer, more authentic, life. On the TV show I paid homage to the communities I belong to by being myself at all times and creating camp, colourful, indulgent bakes inspired by my own life experiences.

Fun fact: I wore a different coloured T-shirt from the Progress Pride flag on each episode!

Since appearing on *Bake Off*, life has been a whirlwind of adventures, from walking red carpets, to winning an LGBTQ+ Champion award. However, the thing I am most proud of is meeting so many incredible people from different communities all over the world who told me how proud they were of me and how they felt represented during my time on *Bake Off*.

For this reason, when I was first approached to write a cookbook I knew I wanted it to be a celebration of Pride.

Before I even started thinking about the contents of this book, I already knew what I *didn't* want it to become. I didn't want to just create a Pride-themed baking book filled with generic, rainbow-coloured bakes without any deeper meaning. Instead, after a lot of research and self-reflection, I put as much of my time and effort into the chapters, flavours and LGBTQ+ stories within this book as I have in my heart.

I want you, the reader, to come on a journey with me as we explore the history of Pride, what Pride means to me personally, what Pride means today, and why it's still so important – all through the art of baking.

This book isn't exclusive to members of marginalised communities. It's for everyone who knows and loves somebody from these communities, for allies who support these communities and for those who want to learn more about them, and me, and the stories we have to tell.

Across six Pride-inspired chapters, we'll learn about LGBTQ+ History in the Baking, learn to Cele-Bake Ourselves and all that makes us unique, Share the Love by baking for the ones we love, explore the theme of Home Pride, and get party-ready with Brunch Bakes and Pride Party showstoppers.

The chapters contain 100 sweet, Pride-inspired recipes for bakes, ranging from simple cookies to stunning celebration cakes suitable for a range of skills. But, even more importantly, the recipes are designed to be FUN!

So put on your apron, get inspired, have fun and bake me ... and yourself ... PROUD!

*hunbun
noun (plural hunbuns)

An affectionate term for a loved one, derived from honey bunch/honey bunny.

HISTORY

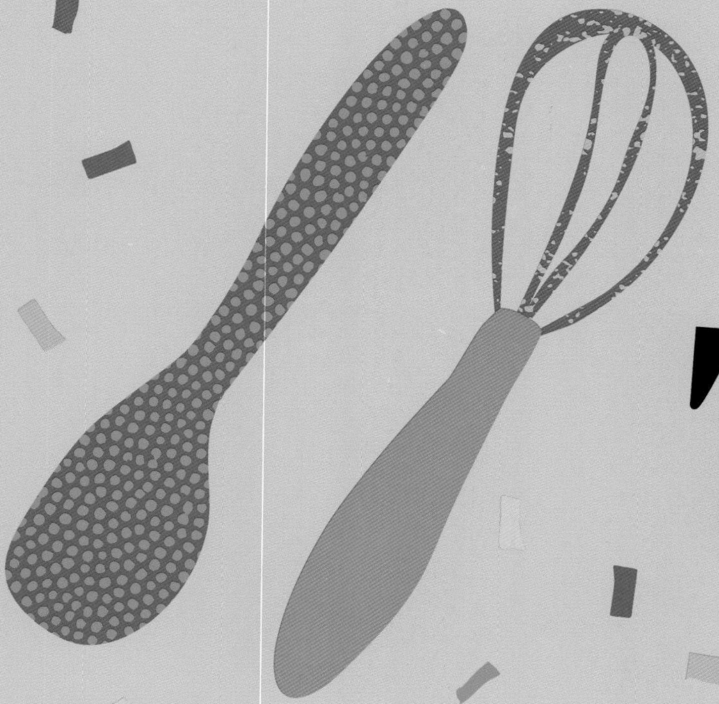

IN THE

BAKING

This light, fragrant cake consists of lavender-flavoured sponge with lemon curd and honey buttercream filling. The piped floral decoration contains a hidden message. This relates to a time in history when LGBTQ+ people would have to use subtle and secret ways to express themselves, including wearing certain types of flowers, including daffodils, lavender, poppies and violets.

SEMI-NAKED FLOWER CAKE

LAVENDER SPONGE

300ml (10½fl oz) full-cream (whole) milk
8g (¼oz) dried organic food-grade lavender
175g (6oz) unsalted butter, room temperature
325g (11½oz) caster (superfine) sugar
3 teaspoons vegetable oil
½ teaspoon white vinegar
1 tablespoon natural vanilla extract
4 large egg whites, room temperature
350g (12oz) cake flour
2 teaspoons baking powder
1 teaspoon bicarbonate of soda (baking soda)

1. Combine the milk and lavender in a jug and set aside for 1 hour to infuse. Strain into a large bowl and set aside.

2. Preheat the oven to 175°C (345°F). Grease the base and sides of four 15cm (6 inch) round cake tins and line the bases with baking paper.

3. In a stand mixer with the paddle attachment, beat the butter, gradually adding the sugar, a tablespoon at a time, until the sugar is fully incorporated and the mixture is pale and creamy.

4. Add the oil, vinegar and vanilla and mix until combined.

5. Whisk the egg whites and lavender-infused milk in a large bowl to combine.

6. Place the flour, baking powder and bicarbonate of soda in a separate large bowl, and whisk briefly to combine.

7. Sift one-third of the flour mixture over the butter mixture and fold it in using a spatula.

8. Add one-third of the lavender-infused milk mixture and mix with a spatula to combine.

9. Repeat steps 7 and 8 until all the flour mixture and lavender-infused milk are used.

10. Transfer the mixture to the tins, level the surface, then bake for 20 minutes until a skewer inserted into the cakes comes out clean.

11. Leave the cakes to cool in the tins for 20 minutes, then transfer to a wire rack to cool completely.

LAVENDER SOAK

90ml (3fl oz) water
90g (3¼oz) caster (superfine) sugar
5 teaspoons dried organic food-grade lavender

1. Combine all the ingredients in a small saucepan over high heat and bring to the boil. Reduce the heat to medium and simmer for 5 minutes.

2. Strain the mixture into a small bowl and set aside to cool.

LEMON CURD

130g (4½oz) caster (superfine) sugar
zest and juice of 2 lemons
3 large egg yolks, room temperature
30g (1oz) unsalted butter, cubed

1 Combine all the ingredients in a medium saucepan over medium heat. Stirring constantly, bring to the boil, cook for around 30 seconds, then remove from the heat.

2 Cover with plastic wrap touching the surface of the curd, to prevent a skin forming, then set aside to cool.

HONEY BUTTERCREAM

4 large egg whites, room temperature
220g (7¾oz) caster (superfine) sugar
360g (12¾oz) unsalted butter, cubed
60ml (2fl oz) runny honey

1 Place the egg whites and sugar in a glass or metal bowl sitting on top of a pan of simmering water, ensuring the water is not touching the base of the bowl. Whisk constantly until the mixture reaches 70°C (150°F) on a sugar thermometer.

2 Transfer to a stand mixer with the whisk attachment and whisk on medium–high for 10 minutes.

3 Change to the paddle attachment. Mixing on medium speed, add the butter, a cube at a time, making sure the butter is fully incorporated after each addition. Add the honey and mix until the buttercream is smooth and fluffy.

4 Transfer two-thirds of the buttercream into a piping bag with a medium nozzle. Set the remaining buttercream aside.

TO ASSEMBLE

1 Use a cake wire or serrated knife to level the tops of the sponges.

2 Place the first sponge in the centre of a cake board or serving plate and drizzle it with one-quarter of the lavender soak.

3 Using the buttercream in the piping bag, pipe honey buttercream over the top of the cake in a thin layer. Pipe a slightly higher border around the edge of the cake to act as a dam to stop the lemon curd from leaking out when you add it.

4 Spread one-third of the lemon curd in the centre of the buttercream in an even layer.

5 Place the second sponge on top and repeat steps 3 and 4.

6 Place the third sponge on top and repeat steps 3 and 4.

7 Place the final sponge on top and drizzle it with the remaining lavender soak.

8 Use the remaining buttercream to create a semi-naked look by piping a small amount of buttercream around the side and on top of the cake, using a cake scraper to smooth it out, ensuring the sponge is exposed in places (see photograph).

TO DECORATE

green, yellow, purple, blue and red gel food colouring

1 Divide the reserved buttercream evenly among five bowls. To the first bowl add ¼ teaspoon of green and ⅛ teaspoon of yellow colouring to make a yellow-green. To the second bowl add ¼ teaspoon of purple and ⅛ teaspoon of blue colouring to make a purple-blue. To the third bowl add ¼ teaspoon of purple colouring. To the fourth bowl add ¼ teaspoon of yellow colouring. To the fifth bowl add ¼ teaspoon of red colouring.

2 Transfer the green buttercream into a piping bag with a small plain nozzle.

3 Transfer the remaining coloured buttercreams into individual piping bags with petal piping nozzles.

4 Using the green buttercream, pipe vertical lines of varying heights on the entire side of the cake, about 2cm (¾ inch) apart, to represent the stems of the flowers.

5 Pipe the leaves, petals and centres of the poppies, lavender, daffodils and violets using the colourful buttercreams (see photograph).

6 Store in the fridge for up to 3 days. Serve at room temperature.

Inspired by the classic ruby slippers worn by Judy Garland in *The Wizard of Oz*, these cupcakes have a vanilla and strawberry sponge base with strands of strawberry jelly throughout. They are topped with sweet buttercream as yellow as the road to Oz and an edible glitter bow plucked straight from Dorothy's shoes.

RUBY SLIPPER CUPCAKES

VANILLA & STRAWBERRY CUPCAKES

1 large egg, room temperature
30ml (1fl oz) water
1 teaspoon vanilla bean paste
75g (2½oz) caster (superfine) sugar
50ml (1½fl oz) vegetable oil
100g (3½oz) plain (all-purpose) flour
½ teaspoon baking powder
30g (1oz) sour cream
1½ teaspoons strawberry jelly (gelatine dessert) powder

1   Preheat the oven to 180°C (350°F). Line six holes of a muffin tin with paper cases.

2   In a stand mixer with the whisk attachment, whisk the egg, water, vanilla and sugar on high speed for 5 minutes. While whisking, gradually pour in the oil and mix until combined.

3   Combine the flour and baking powder in a bowl, then sift half of this mixture over the wet ingredients and fold it in using a spatula. Add the sour cream and fold it in. Sift the remaining flour mixture over the top and fold it in using a spatula.

4   Place 1 tablespoon of cake batter in the bottom of each paper case and sprinkle each with ⅛ teaspoon of strawberry jelly powder. Top each with ½ tablespoon of cake batter and another ⅛ teaspoon of jelly powder. Top with another ½ tablespoon of cake batter.

5   Bake for 15 minutes until a toothpick inserted into the cakes comes out clean. Cool for a few minutes in the tin, then transfer to a wire rack to cool completely.

YELLOW BRICK ROAD BUTTERCREAM

150g (5½oz) unsalted butter, room temperature
1 teaspoon vanilla bean paste
150g (5½oz) condensed milk
¼ teaspoon yellow gel food colouring
1½ teaspoons lemon jelly (gelatine dessert) powder
2 tablespoons water

1   In a stand mixer with the paddle attachment, beat the butter until pale and creamy. Add the vanilla, condensed milk and food colouring and mix until combined and the colour is even.

2   Soak the jelly powder in the water in a microwave-safe bowl for 10 minutes.

3   Heat the bowl in the microwave on High for 5 seconds to melt the jelly powder.

4   Mixing on medium–high speed, add the melted jelly to the butter mixture and mix to combine.

5   Transfer the buttercream to a piping bag with a star nozzle.

RED GLITTER BOWS
60g (2¼oz) red fondant icing
food-grade red glitter powder

1 Place the cupcakes on a serving plate.

2 Pipe the buttercream on top of the cupcakes in a swirl.

3 Create six bows by pressing the fondant icing into 6cm (2½ inch) bow-shaped silicone moulds (or make a template from white card).

4 Trim the excess fondant icing from the top, then press the bows out of the moulds.

5 Place the bows on top of the cupcakes.

6 Sprinkle the cupcakes and bows with the red glitter.

7 Store in an airtight container at room temperature for up to 48 hours.

JANUSZ SAYS

DID YOU KNOW?
As history progressed, queer people found more modern ways of identifying fellow members of the community, such as asking whether somebody was 'a friend of Dorothy' – a nod to Gay icon Judy Garland's role as Dorothy in The Wizard of Oz, *who wore the iconic ruby slippers.*

SERVES 8–10

This cake, consisting of layers of gingery biscuit and vanilla and orange cream cheese frosting, is inspired by the Stonewall riots. The event triggered a global movement in LGBTQ+ activism. Because of the refrigeration time, this recipe is best made a day ahead.

STONEWALL CHEESECAKE STACK

GINGER BISCUIT BASE

60g (2¼oz) ginger nut biscuits (ginger snaps), crushed to a crumb consistency
20g (¾oz) unsalted butter, melted and cooled

1 Preheat the oven to 180°C (350°F). Line two loaf (bar) tins with baking paper – leave some overhang to help you remove the cakes from the tins.

2 In a bowl, mix the crushed biscuits with the melted butter.

3 Divide the biscuit mixture evenly between the tins, pressing it in firmly.

4 Place the tins in the freezer for 10 minutes.

5 Remove from the freezer and bake for 10 minutes. Remove from the oven and set aside to cool completely. Leave the oven on.

CHEESECAKE

400g (14oz) cream cheese, room temperature
100g (3½oz) sour cream, room temperature
125g (4½oz) caster (superfine) sugar
1 tablespoon orange zest
1 tablespoon orange juice, room temperature
2 teaspoons natural vanilla extract
2 large eggs, room temperature

1 In a large bowl, place the cream cheese, sour cream, sugar, orange zest, orange juice and vanilla. Whisk until combined.

2 In a separate bowl, whisk the eggs just for a couple of seconds – do not whip them. Add the egg to the cream cheese mixture and whisk just until combined.

3 Divide the mixture evenly between the tins and level the surface.

4 Place both tins into a large roasting tin and pour in boiling water to reach halfway up the sides of the loaf tins.

5 Return to the oven and bake for 5 minutes. Reduce the temperature to 120°C (235°F) and bake for a further 20 minutes.

6 Switch off the oven and leave the cheesecakes in the oven for 2 hours.

7 Remove from the oven and refrigerate in the tins for 12 hours.

VANILLA & ORANGE CREAM CHEESE FROSTING

90g (3¼oz) unsalted butter, room temperature
200g (7oz) icing (confectioners') sugar, sifted
1 teaspoon natural vanilla extract
1 tablespoon orange zest
10 drops of red gel food colouring
4 drops of yellow gel food colouring
2 drops of brown gel food colouring
150g (5½oz) cream cheese, room temperature

1. In a stand mixer with the paddle attachment, beat the butter until pale and creamy. While mixing, add the sugar, a tablespoon at a time, until fully incorporated.

2. Add the vanilla, orange zest and food colourings and mix until combined and the colour is even.

3. Add the cream cheese and mix until combined and the colour is even.

TO ASSEMBLE

10 pieces of white card
non-toxic coloured pens
10 toothpicks
sticky tape

1. Remove the cheesecakes from the tins using the overhanging baking paper to help you.

2. Place one cheesecake on a serving plate. Cover the top of the cake with one-fifth of the frosting, then place the other cheesecake on top.

3. Cover the cake stack with the remaining frosting, smoothing it over the top and sides.

4. Cut out signs from the card and write your protest messages – make them colourful and use a variety of sizes and shapes. Attach them to the toothpicks with sticky tape, then insert them into the top of the cake (see photograph).

5. Store in the fridge for up to 3 days. Serve at room temperature.

JANUSZ SAYS

DID YOU KNOW?

You cannot talk about the Stonewall riots without mentioning Marsha P. Johnson.

Marsha was a formidable LGBTQ+ activist and self-proclaimed drag queen who was one of many members of the community fighting that night, and consequent nights, against the ongoing, unjust treatment of queer people in New York City. It's commonly said that Marsha 'threw the first brick' at Stonewall. Although this claim has been disputed, she has become synonymous with the Stonewall movement and continued fighting for LGBTQ+ rights, particularly the rights of trans and LGBTQ+ people of colour, until her untimely death in 1992.

History in the Baking

MAKES 20

Similar to a British scone, Welsh cakes are a sweet treat, typically pan-fried in lard. My heart-shaped, classic Welsh cake recipe is in honour of one of my favourite stories in LGBTQ+ history – when miners and gay activists united in 1984–85.

WELSH PRIDE CAKES

50g (1¾oz) lard, cubed, plus 25g (1oz) extra for frying
50g (1¾oz) unsalted butter, room temperature, cubed
225g (8oz) plain (all-purpose) flour, plus extra to dust
80g (2¾oz) caster (superfine) sugar
½ teaspoon baking powder
¼ teaspoon ground cinnamon
¼ teaspoon ground nutmeg
pinch each of ground ginger, allspice, ground cloves and ground cardamom
60g (2¼oz) dried cranberries, halved
icing (confectioners') sugar, sifted, to dust

1 Combine all the ingredients, except the icing sugar, in a stand mixer with the paddle attachment and mix on low speed until a soft dough forms.

2 On a floured work surface, roll out the dough until it is 2cm (¾ inch) thick.

3 Using an 8cm (3¼ inch) heart-shaped cookie cutter, cut out 20 hearts.

4 Heat the extra lard in a large frying pan over medium heat and fry the cakes for 2½–3 minutes on each side until golden brown.

5 Serve immediately, dusted with icing sugar.

6 Eat immediately while hot, or allow to cool and store in an airtight container at room temperature for up to 3 days.

JANUSZ SAYS

DID YOU KNOW?
In 1984–85, during the Welsh miners' strike, a group of Lesbian and Gay activists in London formed an unlikely alliance with a group of Welsh mining communities. Realising they were facing similar treatment by the British government, the activists formed the 'Lesbians and Gays Support the Miners' (LGSM) group to raise awareness and show support for the miners. To show their gratitude, the Welsh miners and their families joined the front of the 1985 London Pride march and went on to support the call for Lesbian and Gay equality.

In 2014 the movie Pride *was released, which celebrated this remarkable event.*

David Bowie was one of the first faces of the gender-bending movement in pop culture and is somebody who still inspires fashion, music ... and now food! These 'red choux' eclairs are filled with a blue curaçao custard and are decorated with a lightning bolt of marzipan. So forget gender norms, pick up a red choux and dance the blues.

DAVID BOWIE 'RED CHOUX' ECLAIRS

'RED CHOUX' ECLAIRS

65g (2¼oz) unsalted butter
125ml (4fl oz) water
¼ teaspoon red gel food colouring
75g (2½oz) plain (all-purpose) flour
pinch of salt
2 large eggs, room temperature

1. Preheat the oven to 190°C (375°F). Grease a baking tray and line it with baking paper.

2. Combine the butter, water and food colouring in a small saucepan over medium–high heat, and bring to the boil. Add the flour and salt and quickly mix using a spatula to combine. The dough is ready when it forms a shiny ball and is no longer sticking to the bottom of the pan. Remove the pan from the heat and set aside to cool for a few minutes.

3. In a bowl, whisk the eggs until frothy.

4. While beating the dough, gradually add the egg mixture to the dough in the saucepan and mix to combine.

5. Transfer the dough to a piping bag with a French star nozzle and pipe 10 x 10cm (4 inch) eclairs onto the tray.

6. Bake for 30 minutes. Open the oven door and poke two holes in each bun with a skewer. Close the oven door and bake for a further 5 minutes. Let the eclairs cool completely inside the oven with the door open.

BLUE CURAÇAO CUSTARD

3 large egg yolks, room temperature
100g (3½oz) caster (superfine) sugar
1 teaspoon vanilla bean paste
12g (⅓oz) plain (all-purpose) flour
12g (⅓oz) cornflour (cornstarch)
100ml (3½fl oz) full-cream (whole) milk
250g (9oz) double (thick) cream
½ teaspoon blue gel food colouring
75ml (2¼fl oz) blue curaçao
1 platinum gelatine leaf
100ml (3½fl oz) water

1. In a medium bowl, whisk the egg yolks, sugar, vanilla, flour and cornflour until combined.

2. Combine the milk, 100g (3½oz) of the cream, the food colouring and blue curaçao in a medium saucepan over medium heat and stir until almost boiling.

3. Add half the milk mixture to the egg yolk mixture, whisking constantly.

4. Return the mixture to the pan and whisk constantly until it boils and thickens.

5. Transfer to a bowl, cover with plastic wrap touching the surface of the custard, to prevent a skin forming, then refrigerate to cool.

6. Soak the gelatine in the water in a microwave-safe bowl for 10 minutes.

7. In a mixing bowl, whip the remaining cream until soft peaks form.

8. Squeeze the excess moisture from the gelatine, then melt it in the microwave on High for 5 seconds.

9. Add the gelatine to the whipped cream and whip for 10 seconds.

10. Whisk the cooled custard until softened.

11. Use a spatula to fold the whipped cream into the custard. Transfer to a piping bag with a long, plain nozzle and refrigerate until ready to use.

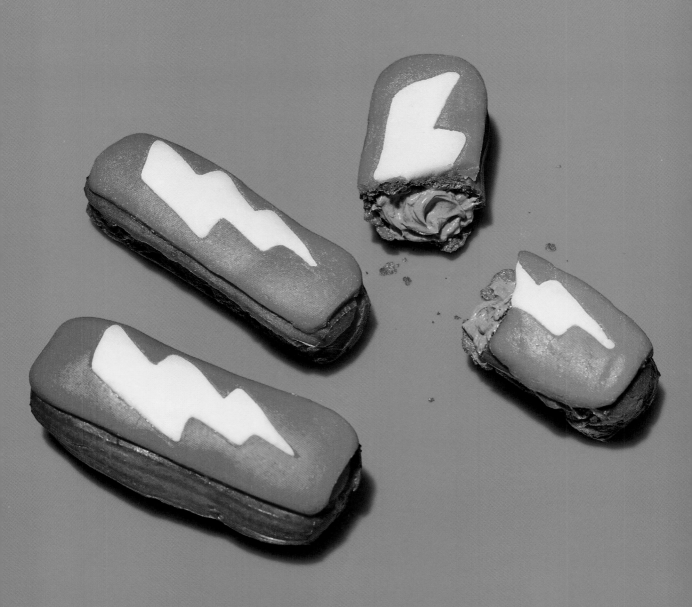

MARZIPAN LIGHTNING BOLT

200g (7oz) marzipan
½ teaspoon red gel food colouring
¼ teaspoon yellow gel food colouring
icing (confectioners') sugar, sifted, to dust

1   Combine 125g (4½oz) of the marzipan and the red food colouring in a stand mixer with the paddle attachment and mix until well combined. Remove from the mixer and clean the bowl.

2   Combine the remaining marzipan and the yellow food colouring in the stand mixer with the paddle attachment and mix until well combined.

3   On a work surface dusted with icing sugar, roll out both pieces of marzipan until they are 5mm (¼ inch) thick.

4   Cut the red marzipan into rectangles the same size as the eclairs.

5   Cut out a lightning bolt-shaped hole from the centre of the rectangles. (You could use a small lightning bolt-shaped cookie cutter or cut a template out of card, so you can match the shapes to the holes.)

6   Cut out lightning bolts from the yellow marzipan and use to fill the holes in the red marzipan.

TO ASSEMBLE

2 teaspoons smooth apricot jam

1   Pipe the custard into the eclairs gently so as not to overfill them.

2   Place the marzipan on top of the eclairs and brush with a small amount of apricot jam for shine. Enjoy immediately and be fabulous!

3   Store in an airtight container in the fridge for up to 3 days.

JANUSZ SAYS

David Bowie famously painted his face with the lightning bolt – or 'flash' – decoration for his iconic character Aladdin Sane.

MAKES 24

These cookies really are bursting with pride. When baked, the dark cookie topping cracks to reveal a fun, colourful centre as vibrant as you are!

BURSTING WITH PRIDE COOKIES

COLOURFUL WHITE CHOCOLATE COOKIES

50g (1¾oz) white chocolate, chopped
100g (3½oz) unsalted butter, room temperature
100g (3½oz) caster (superfine) sugar
100g (3½oz) soft brown sugar
1 large egg, room temperature
1 tablespoon natural vanilla extract
240g (8¾oz) plain (all-purpose) flour
1 teaspoon baking powder
1 teaspoon each of red, orange, yellow, green, blue and purple gel food colouring

DARK COOKIE TOPPING

60g (2¼oz) unsalted butter, room temperature
70g (2½oz) icing (confectioners') sugar, sifted
70g (2½oz) plain (all-purpose) flour
2 tablespoons pure unsweetened cocoa powder
1 teaspoon black gel food colouring

1   For the colourful cookies, heat the white chocolate in the microwave on High in 15-second bursts, stirring after each burst, until melted.

2   In a stand mixer with the paddle attachment, beat the butter and sugars until pale and creamy.

3   Add the melted chocolate to the bowl and mix until combined. Add the egg and vanilla and mix until combined. Sift the flour and baking powder over the mixture and mix until a soft dough forms.

4   Divide the dough into six equal portions and place in separate bowls. Add a different food colouring to each portion and mix until well combined and the colours are even.

5   Combine all the different-coloured dough portions briefly by hand to create a marbled effect.

6   Roll the dough into 24 walnut-sized balls. Flatten the balls slightly and place them on a greased baking tray lined with baking paper.

7   Refrigerate for 20 minutes.

8   Preheat the oven to 190°C (375°F).

9   For the dark cookie topping, in a stand mixer with the paddle attachment, mix all the ingredients on low speed until a thick paste forms.

10   Transfer the paste to a work surface and roll it out between two pieces of plastic wrap until it is about 2mm (⅟₁₆ inch) thick.

11   Using an 8cm (3¼ inch) round cookie cutter, cut out 24 discs – large enough to cover the colourful cookies.

12   Remove the colourful cookies from the fridge and cover each one with a disc of the dark dough. (You can cut the dough balls in half and combine different colours for an even more spectacular effect, if you prefer.)

13   Using a sharp knife, score the black topping with a jagged, tiger stripe-like pattern to allow the topping to crack open during baking and reveal the colours underneath.

14   Bake the cookies for 11 minutes. Leave to cool on the tray for 5 minutes, then transfer to a wire rack to cool completely.

15   Store in an airtight container for up to 5 days.

MAKES 12

Freddie Mercury was not only a rock star, he was (and remains) a symbol of self-Pride today. I want to help others channel a bit more Freddie with these banana and cardamom biscuits shaped like the iconic Mercury moustache. I encourage everyone to try them on for size and live your own life unapologetically, just like Freddie.

FREDDIE MERCURY MOUSTACHE BISCUITS

BANANA & CARDAMOM BISCUITS

125g (4½oz) plain (all-purpose) flour
50g (1¾oz) unsalted butter, room temperature, cubed
1½ tablespoons double (thick) cream
25g (1oz) icing (confectioners') sugar, sifted
1 teaspoon banana extract
½ teaspoon ground cardamom
pinch of salt
¼ teaspoon yellow gel food colouring

1 Combine all the ingredients in a stand mixer with the paddle attachment and mix on high speed until a dough forms.

2 Wrap the dough in plastic wrap and refrigerate for 30 minutes.

3 Remove the dough from the fridge and let it rest for 10 minutes.

4 On a floured work surface, roll out the dough until 5–10mm (¼–½ inch) thick.

5 Using a moustache-shaped cookie cutter, about 12cm (4½ inches) long (or a knife and a template made from card), cut out iconic Freddie moustache shapes. Place the biscuits on the baking tray.

6 Place the tray in the freezer for 10 minutes.

7 Meanwhile, preheat the oven to 180°C (350°F). Grease a baking tray and line it with baking paper.

8 Remove the biscuits from the freezer and bake for 9 minutes. Leave to cool on the tray for 5 minutes, then transfer to a wire rack to cool completely.

MOUSTACHE DECORATION

25g (1oz) dark chocolate (80% cocoa solids), chopped
black gel food colouring

1 Heat the chocolate in the microwave on High in 20-second bursts, stirring after each burst, until melted.

2 Add two drops of black food colouring to the melted chocolate and stir until combined and the colour is even.

3 Use a pastry brush to paint the black chocolate onto the biscuits, creating a hair-like effect.

4 Allow the chocolate to set completely before handing out your Freddie Mercury moustache biscuits. Hold them in place for a great photo opportunity and go on living life a little more loud and proud!

5 Store in an airtight container for up to 5 days.

JANUSZ SAYS

DID YOU KNOW?
The banana and cardamom flavours were chosen as they are popular in Freddie's birth place of Zanzibar!

MAKES 8

It's hard to imagine a time and place where being yourself could see you imprisoned. These vegan fruit-and-nut oat bars are as filling and delicious as they are simple to make. While there's still a way to go globally, these dairy and gluten 'free-from' bars were inspired by the beginning of the decriminalisation of homosexuality.

FREE-FROM BARS

200g (7oz) gluten-free oats
350g (12oz) vegan gluten-free
  condensed milk
100g (3½oz) dried cranberries
30g (1oz) goji berries
100g (3½oz) pecan nuts,
  chopped
60g (2¼oz) desiccated (dried
  shredded) coconut
50g (1¾oz) sunflower seeds
50g (1¾oz) pepitas (pumpkin
  seeds)
pinch of salt

1   Preheat the oven to 140°C (275°F). Line a 20cm (8 inch) square cake tin with baking paper.

2   Blitz the oats in a food processor for 5 seconds.

3   Bring the condensed milk to the boil in a saucepan over medium–high heat. Remove the pan from the heat, add the remaining ingredients and mix until combined.

4   Transfer the mixture to the tin and distribute it evenly over the base. Do not press the mixture down as it will harden after baking. Bake for 45 minutes.

5   Remove the tray from the oven and leave to cool for 15 minutes. Cut into eight bars in the tin. Leave to cool completely, then remove from the tin.

6   Store in an airtight container for up to 5 days.

JANUSZ SAYS

DID YOU KNOW?
The first western European country to decriminalise homosexual acts was France in 1791.

MAKES 1 LOAF

This sweet, light and fluffy rainbow milk loaf is inspired by the original LGBTQ+ Pride flag created by Gilbert Baker in 1978. This loaf is best served warm with butter – it's also perfect to use for Rainbow Cloud French Toast (see page 173).

RAINBOW MILK LOAF

700g (1lb 9oz) strong flour, sifted
500ml (17fl oz) full-cream (whole) milk
70g (2½oz) caster (superfine) sugar
1 teaspoon salt
12g (⅓oz) active dried yeast
2 egg yolks, room temperature
85g (3oz) unsalted butter, room temperature, plus extra for greasing
¼ teaspoon each of red, orange, yellow, green, blue and purple gel food colouring

1 Combine 100g (3½oz) of the flour and 240ml (8fl oz) of the milk in a small saucepan over medium–high heat and cook for 30 seconds, stirring constantly.

2 Transfer to a bowl, cover and refrigerate for a minimum of 4 hours.

3 In a stand mixer with the dough hook attachment, combine the remaining flour, the milk/flour mixture, the remaining milk, the sugar, salt, yeast and egg yolks. Mix on medium speed for 10 minutes until fully combined. Add the butter and mix for a further 5 minutes.

4 Cover the dough and leave to prove in a warm place for 90 minutes.

5 Divide the dough into six equal portions.

6 Put one portion in the bowl of a stand mixer with the dough hook attachment with one of the food colourings and mix until well combined and the colour is even. Clean the bowl and repeat with the remaining dough and food colourings.

7 Grease and line a 34 x 13.5 x 12cm (13½ x 5¼ x 4½ inch) loaf (bar) tin with baking paper – leave some overhang to help you remove the cake from the tin.

8 Grease your hands and work surface with butter. Roll out each dough portion into a rectangle to fit the bottom of the loaf tin.

9 Layer the coloured dough rectangles on top of each other in the loaf tin – from top to bottom: red, orange, yellow, green, blue and purple.

10 Cover the dough and leave to prove in a warm place for 40 minutes.

11 Preheat the oven to 190°C (375°F).

12 Uncover the tin and bake for 30 minutes until the loaf has a nice golden brown crust. Leave to cool in the tin.

13 Store in an airtight container for up to 2 days.

JANUSZ SAYS

DID YOU KNOW?
Gilbert Baker was asked by the iconic American political activist Harvey Milk to come up with a symbol of Pride for the community. The rainbow flag debuted in 1978 and is still used today throughout the world as a symbol of LGBTQ+ Pride.

These red velvet, ribbon-shaped biscuits are a small tribute to some of the bravest people from our community who lost their lives or fought the fight during the HIV/AIDS epidemic. They inspired generations of the LGBTQ+ community to fight for their rights, and helped to end the stigma surrounding people living with HIV/AIDS today.

RED VELVET RIBBON BISCUITS

RED VELVET BISCUITS

50g (1¾oz) unsalted butter, room temperature
50g (1¾oz) caster (superfine) sugar
1 teaspoon vanilla bean paste
1 teaspoon white vinegar
¼ teaspoon red gel food colouring
25g (1oz) cream cheese, room temperature
¼ teaspoon bicarbonate of soda (baking soda)
90g (3¼oz) plain (all-purpose) flour
10g (⅓oz) cornflour (cornstarch)
1 tablespoon pure unsweetened cocoa powder

1 In a stand mixer with the paddle attachment, beat the butter and sugar until pale and creamy. Add the vanilla, vinegar, food colouring and cream cheese and mix until well combined and the colour is even.

2 Sift the dry ingredients over the butter mixture and mix until a soft dough forms.

3 Wrap the dough in plastic wrap and refrigerate for 60 minutes.

4 Remove the dough from the fridge. On a floured work surface, roll out the dough until 3mm (1⁄16 inch) thick.

5 Using a 7cm (2¾ inch) awareness ribbon-shaped cookie cutter (or a knife and a template made from card), cut out 24 ribbon-shaped cookies.

6 Preheat the oven to 180°C (350°F). Grease a baking tray and line it with baking paper.

7 Place the biscuits on the baking tray and freeze for 15 minutes.

8 Remove the biscuits from the freezer and bake for 9 minutes until slightly golden. Cool on the tray for 5 minutes, then transfer to a wire rack to cool completely.

RED CREAM CHEESE FROSTING

75g (2½oz) unsalted butter, room temperature
100g (3½oz) icing (confectioners') sugar, sifted
1 teaspoon natural vanilla extract
100g (3½oz) cream cheese, room temperature
½ teaspoon red gel food colouring

1 In a stand mixer with the paddle attachment, beat the butter and sugar until pale and creamy. Add the vanilla, cream cheese and food colouring and mix until combined and the colour is even.

2 Transfer the frosting to a piping bag with small plain nozzle.

3 Place the biscuits on a serving plate and pipe the frosting onto the ribbons. Enjoy while reflecting on those that fought so hard.

4 Store in a single layer in an airtight container in the fridge for up to 3 days.

JANUSZ SAYS

DID YOU KNOW?
Thanks to scientific advances, people living with HIV today who are on effective treatment can have an undetectable viral load, meaning they cannot pass the virus on to others.

In the early 1990s the World Health Organization officially declassified homosexuality as a mental illness. These buttery rainbow Viennese biscuits dipped in white chocolate and sprinkles are a reminder to be kind and shine light on those that may feel cloudy – and remember, after rain comes rainbows!

RAINBOW CLOUD BISCUITS

RAINBOW VIENNESE BISCUITS

100g (3½oz) unsalted butter, room temperature
60g (2¼oz) icing (confectioners') sugar, sifted
2 egg yolks, room temperature
2 teaspoons vanilla bean paste
125g (4½oz) plain (all-purpose) flour
⅛ teaspoon each of red, orange, yellow, green, blue and purple gel food colouring

1 Preheat the oven to 180°C (350°F). Grease a baking tray and line it with baking paper.

2 In a stand mixer with the paddle attachment, beat the butter, gradually adding the sugar, a tablespoon at a time, until the mixture is pale and creamy and the sugar is fully incorporated. Add the egg yolks and vanilla and mix until combined. Sift the flour over the butter mixture and gently mix until combined.

3 Divide the dough evenly among six bowls. Add a different food colouring to each portion and mix until well combined and the colours are even.

4 Open out a piping bag and pipe or spoon lines of the different coloured doughs vertically on the inside of the piping bag in rainbow colour order.

5 Attach a star nozzle to the bag and pipe four large rainbows, with a cloud at each end, onto the baking tray.

6 Place in the freezer for 15 minutes.

7 Remove from the freezer and bake for 12 minutes. Transfer to a wire rack to cool.

WHITE CHOCOLATE CLOUDS

60g (2¼oz) white chocolate, chopped
1 teaspoon rainbow sprinkles

1 Heat the white chocolate in the microwave on High in 15-second bursts, stirring after each burst, until melted.

2 Place the rainbow biscuits on a wire rack with a sheet of baking paper underneath.

3 Use the white chocolate to coat the clouds at both ends of each rainbow. Cover the chocolate with sprinkles and leave to set.

4 Store in an airtight container for up to 5 days.

JANUSZ SAYS

DID YOU KNOW?
Although declassifying homosexuality as a mental illness was a huge step forward, LGBTQ+ people are still more likely to suffer from mental health issues due to experiences of discrimination, bullying, isolation or rejection because of their sexuality or gender.

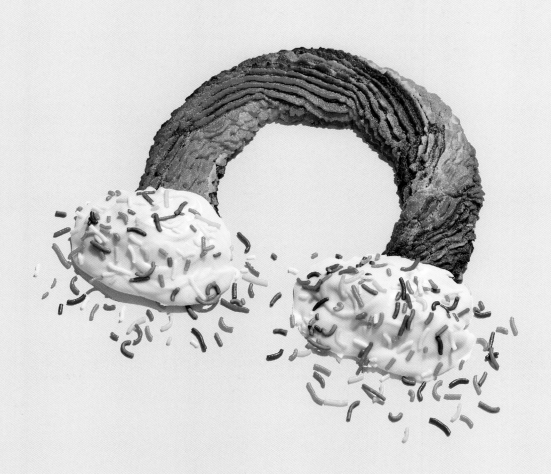

SERVES 30–40

This two-tiered wedding cake celebrates a monumental moment of Pride in LGBTQ+ history – the legalisation of Gay marriage. The bitterness of the baked lemon sponge is sweetened with white chocolate and decorated with a white chocolate buttercream, a rainbow drip, rosettes and balloons. Let's get this party started!

LGBTQ+WEDDING CAKE

BOTTOM TIER LEMON SPONGE

4 organic unwaxed lemons
6 large eggs, room temperature
500g (1lb 2oz) caster (superfine) sugar
1 tablespoon vanilla bean paste
500g (1lb 2oz) unsalted butter, melted and cooled
500g (1lb 2oz) plain (all-purpose) flour
3 teaspoons baking powder
½ teaspoon bicarbonate of soda (baking soda)
40g (1½oz) poppy seeds

TOP TIER LEMON SPONGE

2 organic unwaxed lemons
3 large eggs, room temperature
250g (9oz) caster (superfine) sugar
2 teaspoons vanilla bean paste
250g (9oz) unsalted butter, melted and cooled
250g (9oz) plain (all-purpose) flour
1½ teaspoons baking powder
¼ teaspoon bicarbonate of soda (baking soda)
20g (¾oz) poppy seeds

1   For the bottom tier sponges, place the lemons in a medium saucepan over medium heat with enough water to cover. Cook, covered, for 20 minutes. Remove the lemons from the pan and set aside to cool to room temperature.

2   Cut the lemons in half, remove any seeds, then put all the lemon halves in a food processor and blitz to a smooth purée.

3   Preheat the oven to 180°C (350°F). Grease the base and sides of three round 20cm (8 inch) cake tins and line the bases with baking paper.

4   In a stand mixer with the whisk attachment, whisk the eggs and sugar on high speed until light and fluffy. Add the blended lemons and vanilla and whisk gently to combine. Add the melted butter and whisk to combine.

5   In a separate bowl, combine the flour, baking powder and bicarbonate of soda.

6   Sift the flour mixture over the batter in two batches, folding it in using a spatula after each addition. Add the poppy seeds and gently stir them through the mixture.

7   Divide the batter evenly among the tins, level the surface, then bake for 35 minutes until a toothpick inserted into the cakes comes out clean. Leave to cool in the tins for a few minutes, then transfer to a wire rack to cool completely.

8   Preheat the oven to 180°C (350°F). Grease the base and sides of three round 15cm (6 inch) cake tins and line the bases with baking paper.

9   To make the top tier sponges, repeat steps 2–7 as for the bottom tier sponge, but bake for only 25 minutes.

LEMON CURD

5 egg yolks, room temperature
zest and juice of 2 lemons
80g (2¾oz) caster (superfine)
    sugar
40g (1½oz) unsalted butter

1   Combine all the ingredients in a
    medium saucepan over medium
    heat. Stirring constantly, bring to the
    boil, cook for around 30 seconds,
    then remove from the heat.

2   Cover with plastic wrap touching the
    surface of the curd, to prevent a skin
    forming, then set aside to cool.

WHITE CHOCOLATE BUTTERCREAM

6 large egg whites, room
    temperature
300g (10½oz) caster (superfine)
    sugar
150g (5½oz) white chocolate,
    chopped
500g (1lb 2oz) unsalted butter,
    room temperature, cubed
1 tablespoon natural vanilla extract

1   Place the egg whites and sugar in a
    glass or metal bowl sitting on top of
    a pan of simmering water, ensuring
    the water is not touching the base
    of the bowl. Whisk constantly until
    the mixture reaches 70°C (150°F)
    on a sugar thermometer.

2   Transfer to a stand mixer with the
    whisk attachment and whisk on
    medium–high speed for 15 minutes.

3   Heat the white chocolate in the
    microwave on High in 15-second
    bursts, stirring after each burst,
    until melted.

4   Leave the chocolate to cool, but
    don't let it set.

5   Change the stand mixer to the
    paddle attachment. Mixing on
    medium speed, add the butter,
    a cube at a time, making sure the
    butter is fully incorporated after
    each addition. Mix until the mixture
    is smooth and fluffy. Add the vanilla
    and melted chocolate and mix until
    just combined.

RAINBOW BUTTERCREAM

250g (9oz) unsalted butter, room
    temperature
500g (1lb 2oz) icing
    (confectioners') sugar, sifted
1 teaspoon lemon oil
⅛ teaspoon each of red, orange,
    yellow, green, blue and purple gel
    food colouring

1   In a stand mixer with the paddle
    attachment, beat the butter until pale
    and creamy. While mixing, gradually
    add the sugar, a tablespoon at a
    time, until it is fully incorporated and
    the buttercream is smooth. Add the
    lemon oil and mix to combine.

2   Divide the buttercream evenly
    among six bowls and add a different
    food colouring to each bowl. Mix
    thoroughly until combined and the
    colours are even.

3   Transfer each colour to a separate
    piping bag with a star nozzle.

RAINBOW DRIP

100g (3½oz) double (thick) cream
250g (9oz) white chocolate,
    chopped
2 drops each of red, orange,
    yellow, green, blue and purple gel
    food colouring

1   Heat the cream in a medium
    saucepan over medium–high heat
    until boiling. Remove the pan from
    the heat, add the chocolate and
    leave to sit for 2 minutes, then stir
    until the chocolate is melted and
    the mixture is smooth.

2   Divide the mixture evenly among
    six bowls and add a different
    food colouring to each bowl. Mix
    thoroughly until combined and the
    colours are even. Set aside.

TO ASSEMBLE

cake support set featuring 3 long
  dowels with separator plate
20 small balloons in rainbow
  colours
string
2 large paper straws

1 Place one of the large sponges on a cake board or serving plate. Separate the white chocolate buttercream into two bowls: the first containing two-thirds of the mixture, and the second containing one-third. Also separate the lemon curd into two bowls: the first containing two-thirds of the curd, and the second containing one-third.

2 Spread one-quarter of the larger bowl of buttercream in a thin layer on top. Pipe a higher border of white chocolate buttercream around the edge to act as a dam to stop the lemon curd from leaking out.

3 Spread one-third of the larger bowl of lemon curd inside the border.

4 Top with a second large sponge and repeat with one-quarter of the larger bowl of buttercream and one-third of the larger bowl of curd.

5 Top with the last large sponge and repeat with another one-quarter of the larger bowl of buttercream and the remaining lemon curd.

6 Cover the sides of the cake stack with the remaining buttercream from the larger bowl, smoothing it out with a cake scraper.

7 Refrigerate the cake for at least 1 hour.

8 Repeat the process with the smaller sponges, using the smaller bowls of buttercream and lemon curd.

9 You will need to measure how high your cake will be so you know what length the dowels need to be. Cut the dowels to size, then insert them in the centre of the larger sponge stack with the separator plate on top, to hold the smaller cake stack in place when it is added.

10 Set the smaller cake stack on top of the dowels, in the centre, pushing down until the top stack is flush with the bottom stack.

11 Create a drip effect by spooning just a little of each colour on the top edge of the top cake stack and allowing it to drip down the side. Repeat with the bottom cake stack (see photograph).

12 Using the different-coloured buttercreams, pipe 5cm (2 inch) high rosettes around the edge of the bottom cake stack so that they correspond with the colour of the drip below (see photograph).

13 Inflate the balloons so they are quite small (just bigger than the size of your hand). Tie the balloons together in pairs using a long piece of string, leaving a 20cm (8 inch) tail. Place another pair of balloons on top, crossways. Wrap the string around both pairs of balloons and pull to tighten. Repeat with the remaining balloons. Cut the end of the string, leaving a tail of about 20cm (8 inches). Loop the end around the last balloon pair and tie it off inside the loop to secure it.

14 Poke a hole through each paper straw near the top. Thread one tail of the balloon string through the hole in the straw. Loop the string around the last balloon and make a knot. Trim the excess string. Repeat with the other tail of string. The bunch of balloons will now have two vertical straws at the base. Just before serving, stick the straws into the top of the cake to secure the balloons.

15 If you are planning to transport the cake, you will need to chill it in the fridge. If not, it can remain at room temperature.

16 Store in the fridge, without the cake topper, for up to 3 days. Serve at room temperature.

JANUSZ SAYS

The first same-sex couple in the world to legally marry were Gert Kasteel and Dolf Pasker. They were married in Amsterdam – along with three other couples – just after midnight on 1 April 2001, when the Netherlands became the first country to legalise same-sex marriage.

SERVES 10

This stunning cake consists of genoise sponge soaked in pear juice and amaretto, layered with pieces of pear and a caramel cream filling. It is decorated with alternating dark and milk chocolate drips, and pink, blue and white buttercream swirls representing the Progress Pride flag.

INCLUSIVE PRIDE FLAG PEAR & CARAMEL CAKE

GENOISE SPONGE

4 large eggs, room temperature, separated
130g (4½oz) caster (superfine) sugar
1 tablespoon natural vanilla extract
100g (3½oz) plain (all-purpose) flour
40g (1½oz) cornflour (cornstarch)

1. Preheat the oven to 180°C (350°F). Line the base of two 15cm (6 inch) round cake tins with baking paper.

2. In a stand mixer with the whisk attachment, whisk the egg whites until stiff peaks form. While whisking, gradually add the sugar, a tablespoon at a time, over a period of 5 minutes, until fully incorporated.

3. In a small bowl, combine the egg yolks and vanilla, then add this mixture to the egg whites, whisking on medium speed to combine. In a separate bowl, combine the flour and cornflour.

4. Sift the flour mixture over the egg mixture in three separate batches, folding it in using a spatula after each addition.

5. Divide the mixture evenly between the tins and level the surface.

6. Bake for 25 minutes until golden and a toothpick inserted into the cakes comes out clean.

7. Set aside to cool, then cut the sponges out of the cake tins using a serrated knife.

CARAMEL & PEAR FILLING

200g (7oz) tinned caramel, chilled in the fridge for at least 6 hours
250g (9oz) mascarpone, cold
100g (3½oz) double (thick) cream
1 teaspoon caramel flavouring
415g (14¾oz) tinned pears in light syrup (reserve the syrup)

1. In a stand mixer with the whisk attachment, whisk the chilled caramel, mascarpone, cream and caramel flavouring until smooth, creamy and thick.

2. Transfer the mixture to a piping bag with a plain nozzle.

3. Cut the pears into 5mm (¼ inch) pieces and set aside. Reserve the syrup.

RAINBOW CARAMEL BUTTERCREAM

500g (1lb 2oz) unsalted butter, room temperature
500g (1lb 2oz) condensed milk
2 teaspoons vanilla bean paste
1 teaspoon caramel flavouring
¼ teaspoon each of red, orange, yellow, green, blue, purple, pink and baby blue gel food colouring

1. In a stand mixer with the paddle attachment, beat the butter until pale and creamy. While mixing, add the condensed milk and flavourings and mix until combined.

2. Divide the buttercream evenly among nine bowls. Colour each portion with a different food colouring, but leave the ninth plain.

3. Transfer the red, orange, yellow, green, blue and purple buttercreams to disposable piping bags and cut the ends off.

4. Transfer the pink, baby blue and plain buttercreams to piping bags with star nozzles.

CHOCOLATE DRIPS

70g (2½oz) double (thick) cream
50g (1¾oz) dark chocolate
(70% cocoa solids), chopped
50g (1¾oz) milk chocolate
(50% cocoa solids), chopped

1 Heat half the cream in a saucepan over medium–high heat until boiling. Remove the pan from the heat. Add the dark chocolate and leave to sit for 2 minutes. Stir until the chocolate is melted and the mixture is smooth.

2 Leave the chocolate to cool but do not let it set.

3 Repeat steps 1 and 2 with the remaining cream and the milk chocolate. Set aside to cool slightly.

PEAR & AMARETTO SOAK

150ml (5fl oz) reserved syrup from the tinned pears used in filling (above)
50ml (1½fl oz) amaretto

1 Combine the reserved pear syrup and amaretto in a bowl.

TO ASSEMBLE

1 Cut the two sponges in half horizontally using a cake wire or a serrated knife, so you have four sponges.

2 Place one of the sponges on a cake board or serving plate. Spoon over one-quarter of the soak. Using one-third of the buttercream, cover the sponge and pipe a 2.5cm (1 inch) high border around the edge of the cake to act as a dam to keep the pear filling in place.

3 Fill the centre of the cake inside the border with one-third of the pear filling.

4 Place the second sponge on top. Add another one-quarter of the soak, another one-third of the buttercream and another one-third of the pear filling.

5 Top with the third sponge, adding another one-quarter of the soak and the remaining buttercream and pear filling.

6 Top with the fourth sponge, adding the remaining soak.

7 Starting from the bottom of the cake, pipe horizontal stripes of the purple, blue, green, yellow, orange and red buttercreams around the side of the cake to create a rainbow effect. Smooth using a cake scraper.

8 Spread a thin layer of red buttercream on top of the cake, smoothing with a palette knife. Refrigerate for 30 minutes.

9 Remove from the fridge. Using a teaspoon, create a drip effect around the side of the cake with the dark and milk chocolate drips.

10 Refrigerate for 30 minutes for the drip to set.

11 Remove from the fridge. Pipe rosettes of baby blue, pink and white buttercream in a circle around the top of the cake.

12 Store the cake in the fridge for up to 24 hours. Serve at room temperature.

JANUSZ SAYS

DID YOU KNOW?

The Progress Pride flag was created in 2018 by non-binary artist and designer Daniel Quasar to bring visibility and awareness to communities often discriminated against within the community. This was achieved by adding a forward-facing arrow to the front of the Pride flag, comprised of white, pink, blue, brown and black stripes. The Progress Pride flag represents transgender, non-binary and marginalised people of colour within the community.

History in the Baking

This fabulous roulade is a homage to the iconic RuPaul who, through mainstream TV, has broken barriers for Queer people by shining a light on the world of drag and showcasing some of the talent the world now recognises. Ru is as sweet and soft as the rolled vanilla sponge in this 'ru-lade', but their wit and clapbacks are as sharp as the strawberry cream within.

RU-LADE PAUL

COLOURFUL PATTERN

1 egg white, room temperature
pinch of salt
2 tablespoons caster (superfine) sugar
1 teaspoon vegetable oil
20g (¾oz) plain (all-purpose) flour
two drops each of pink and purple gel food colouring

1 Grease and line a Swiss roll (jelly roll) tin with baking paper.

2 In a stand mixer with the whisk attachment, whisk the egg white until stiff peaks form. Add the salt and sugar and whisk for a further minute. Add the oil and mix to combine. Sift the flour over the mixture and gently fold it in using a spatula.

3 Divide the mixture evenly between two bowls and add the pink food colouring to one bowl and purple to the other. Fold each mixture with a spatula until combined and the colours are even.

4 Transfer the batter into two separate piping bags with small plain nozzles.

5 Pipe a pattern onto the papered tin – I piped a line of false lashes in alternating colours along the ru-lade, then a line of hearts in alternating colours. Repeat the pattern around the border.

6 Place the tin in the freezer for 30 minutes.

ROULADE

3 large eggs, room temperature, separated
pinch of salt
80g (2¾oz) caster (superfine) sugar
1 teaspoon vanilla bean paste
80g (2¾oz) plain (all-purpose) flour
½ teaspoon baking powder

1 Preheat the oven to 180°C (350°F).

2 In a stand mixer with the whisk attachment, whisk the egg whites until frothy. Add the salt, then whisk until stiff peaks form. While whisking, gradually add the sugar, a tablespoon at a time, until fully incorporated. Add the egg yolks and vanilla and whisk until combined.

3 Sift the flour and baking powder over the egg mixture and fold them in using a spatula.

4 Remove the tin from the freezer, add the roulade mixture to the tin, then level the surface.

5 Bake for 10 minutes until golden and the sponge springs back when pressed with a finger.

6 Remove from the oven and invert the hot cake onto a clean tea towel (dish towel). Gently peel off the baking paper.

7 With the help of the tea towel, invert the cake onto another clean tea towel. Starting from a short end, roll up the sponge inside the tea towel. Leave to cool for 30 minutes.

STRAWBERRY CREAM

2 platinum gelatine leaves
100ml (3½fl oz) cold water
200g (7oz) strawberries
25g (1oz) caster (superfine) sugar
2 tablespoons lemon juice
250g (9oz) double (thick) cream
100g (3½oz) mascarpone
40g (1½oz) icing (confectioners')
   sugar, sifted

1 Soak the gelatine in the water for
   10 minutes.

2 Combine the strawberries, caster
   sugar and lemon juice in a saucepan
   over high heat and cook until the
   strawberries are soft and starting
   to break up. Remove the pan from
   the heat.

3 Using a hand-held blender, purée
   the mixture.

4 Squeeze the excess water from
   the gelatine and add the gelatine
   to the strawberry mixture. Mix until
   combined, then set aside to cool to
   room temperature – but the mixture
   must not set.

5 Once the mixture is cool, combine
   the cream, mascarpone and icing
   sugar in a bowl. Whip using hand-
   held electric beaters until soft peaks
   form. Add the cooled strawberry
   mixture and mix to combine – do not
   overmix the mixture as it will lose the
   whipped consistency.

6 Transfer to a piping bag and
   refrigerate for 4 hours.

TO ASSEMBLE

50g (1¾oz) fresh strawberries, cut
   into small pieces

1 Carefully unroll the roulade from the
   tea towel.

2 Spread an even layer of the
   strawberry cream over the top of
   the roulade, leaving a 2.5cm (1 inch)
   border at one short end, then cover
   with the strawberries pieces.

3 Starting from the short end without
   the border, roll the roulade up tightly
   and place on a serving plate with the
   seam facing down.

4 Store, covered, in the fridge for up
   to 48 hours.

CELE -BAKE YOURSELF

Fortune cookies are OUT, affirmation cookies are IN. These sweet, thin, folded rainbow cookies are for giving to those you love. When snapped open they reveal a positive affirmation – a reminder to the recipients of just how special they are.

AFFIRMATION COOKIES

40g (1½oz) egg white, room temperature
1½ tablespoons sunflower oil
½ teaspoon almond essence
1 tablespoon full-cream (whole) milk
70g (2½oz) caster (superfine) sugar
40g (1½oz) plain (all-purpose) flour, sifted
10g (⅓oz) cornflour (cornstarch), sifted
red, orange, yellow, green, blue and purple gel food colouring
vegetable oil, for greasing

1   Write, print and cut out 12 positive affirmations on 6 x 1cm (2½ x ½ inch) strips of paper.

2   Preheat the oven to 150°C (300°F).

3   In a medium bowl, mix the egg white, sunflower oil, almond essence and milk until combined.

4   In a separate large bowl, combine the sugar, flour and cornflour.

5   Add the wet mixture to the dry ingredients and stir with a wooden spoon until combined, being careful not to incorporate too much air into the mixture.

6   Divide the mixture evenly among six small bowls and colour each with one drop of a different food colouring. Mix until well combined and the colours are even.

7   Spread a thin layer of vegetable oil over a silicone baking mat. Add two separate tablespoonfuls of one colour of mixture onto the mat.

8   Using the back of a teaspoon, spread each dollop of mixture out into an 8cm (3¼ inch) disc, then bake for 7 minutes.

9   Remove from the oven and, working quickly, prise the cookies off the mat using a palette knife, place an affirmation message in the centre of each cookie, then fold the cookies in half to create semicircles.

10 Hold the semicircles at each end and, holding the bottom of the cookies over the rim of a glass, press down and bend the cookies to resemble fortune cookies.

11 Gently press the edges of the folded cookies to seal them, then transfer to the holes of a cupcake tray to cool so they don't unfold.

12 Repeat steps 7–11 with the remaining batter to make a total of 12 cookies.

13 Store in an airtight container for up to 7 days.

JANUSZ SAYS

JANUSZ-APPROVED POSITIVE AFFIRMATIONS:
- I am Beyoncé
- I am powerful
- I deserve good things
- I am enough
- I am grateful for the body I have
- I am a joy to be around
- I radiate positivity
- I create magic

Show people you DO give a cr*p by gifting them some fun and delicious unicorn poop! Consisting of a buttery, cream biscuit base, these vibrantly coloured snacks are topped with a raspberry jam-filled marshmallow, and decorated with a unicorn's top dietary intake – rainbow sprinkles!

UNICORN POOP

CREAM BISCUIT BASES
30g (1oz) unsalted butter, cold, cubed
85g (3oz) plain (all-purpose) flour, sifted
25g (1oz) icing (confectioners') sugar, sifted
1½ tablespoons double (thick) cream

1 Place the butter, flour and sugar in a bowl and rub with your fingertips until the texture resembles breadcrumbs. Add the cream and mix until a smooth dough forms.

2 Wrap the dough in plastic wrap and refrigerate for 30 minutes.

3 Remove the dough from the fridge. On a floured work surface, roll out the dough until 5mm (¼ inch) thick.

4 Using a 5cm (2 inch) round cookie cutter, cut out eight circles. Place them on a greased baking tray lined with baking paper.

5 Place the tray in the freezer for 15 minutes.

6 Preheat the oven to 180°C (350°F).

7 Remove the tray from the freezer and bake for 12 minutes. Leave to cool on the tray for 5 minutes, then transfer to a wire rack to cool completely.

MARSHMALLOW
2 platinum gelatine leaves
100ml (3½fl oz) water
1 teaspoon vanilla bean paste
2 large egg whites, room temperature
¼ teaspoon purple gel food colouring
150g (5½oz) caster (superfine) sugar

1 Soak the gelatine in the water for 10 minutes.

2 Place the vanilla, egg whites, food colouring and sugar in a glass or metal bowl sitting on top of a pan of simmering water, ensuring the water is not touching the base of the bowl. Using hand-held electric beaters, whisk on high speed for 10 minutes.

3 Squeeze the excess water from the gelatine and add the gelatine to the pan. Whisk on high speed to combine.

4 Remove the mixture from the heat and leave to cool for 15 minutes.

5 Transfer the mixture to a piping bag with a plain nozzle.

TO ASSEMBLE
4 teaspoons raspberry jam
edible glitter dust spray
rainbow sprinkles

1 Place ½ teaspoon of jam in the centre of each biscuit.

2 Pipe marshmallow on top of each biscuit to resemble 'unicorn poop'.

3 Refrigerate for 15 minutes.

4 Remove from the fridge and spray the unicorn poop with glitter, then scatter the sprinkles over the top.

5 These are best eaten on the day they are made.

SERVES 4

Help me celebrate my favourite animal with these fun, indulgent piggy puddings! With layers of chocolate brownie and rich chocolate mousse, topped with a cookie crumb, this bake is only made better with the cute meringue piggies sitting on top. They'll leave you squealing for more.

CHOCOLATE MUD PIE PIG PUDDINGS

CHOCOLATE BROWNIE

60g (2¼oz) unsalted butter
90g (3¼oz) dark chocolate
   (70% cocoa solids), chopped
90g (3¼oz) soft dark brown sugar
1 tablespoon dark rum (optional)
1 large egg, room temperature
1 large egg yolk, room
   temperature
1 teaspoon vanilla bean paste
20g (¾oz) plain (all-purpose)
   flour

1 Preheat the oven to 170°C (325°F). Line a 20cm (8 inch) square baking tin with baking paper.

2 Melt the butter and chocolate in a medium saucepan over medium–high heat. Add the sugar and whisk until combined. Remove from the heat and allow to cool until only slightly warm.

3 Add the rum (if using) egg, egg yolk and vanilla and whisk until combined. Sift the flour over the egg mixture and mix to combine.

4 Transfer the mixture to the tin and bake for 18 minutes. Leave to cool completely in the tin.

CHOCOLATE MOUSSE

160g (5½oz) dark chocolate
   (70% cocoa solids), chopped
160g (5½oz) aquafaba (see
   Janusz Says on page 50)
35g (1¼oz) icing (confectioners')
   sugar, sifted

1 Heat the chocolate in the microwave on High in 30-second bursts, stirring after each burst, until melted. Leave the chocolate to cool until just warm – do not let it set.

2 In a stand mixer with the whisk attachment, whisk the aquafaba on high speed for 5 minutes, gradually adding the sugar in three batches, and whisking after each addition until fully incorporated.

3 Using a spatula, gently fold the melted chocolate into the whipped aquafaba until no white streaks are visible.

MERINGUE PIGGIES

1 large egg white, room
  temperature
50g (1¾oz) caster (superfine)
  sugar
⅛ teaspoon pink gel food
  colouring
black gel food colouring

1 Preheat the oven to 140°C (275°F).
  Grease a baking tray and line it with
  baking paper.

2 In a stand mixer with the whisk
  attachment, whisk the egg white
  until stiff peaks form. While
  whisking, gradually add the sugar,
  a tablespoon at a time, until fully
  incorporated.

3 Add the pink food colouring and
  continue whisking until the sugar is
  fully incorporated and the mixture
  is an even pink colour.

4 Transfer three-quarters of the
  meringue mixture to a piping
  bag with a plain nozzle. Pipe the
  meringues onto the baking tray into
  shapes that will form the body of
  the pigs – about 4cm (1½ inches) in
  diameter. See the photograph for
  reference but have fun with your
  pig-making!

5 Transfer the remaining meringue
  mixture to a separate disposable
  piping bag and cut a small hole in the
  end. Pipe ears, legs, a tail and a snout
  onto the bodies of your piggies.

6 Bake for 60 minutes, remove
  from the oven and leave to cool
  on the tray.

7 Once cool, peel the pigs off the
  baking paper. Use black food
  colouring on a toothpick to draw
  eyes and snout holes on your pigs.

TO ASSEMBLE

100g (3½oz) chocolate biscuits,
  crushed

1 Cut four circles out of the brownie –
  I used my serving dishes as a cutting
  template – and place the circles in
  the bottom of four serving dishes.

2 Top each brownie with chocolate
  mousse and a thin layer of biscuit
  crumbs, then stand the meringue
  piggies on top, basking in all their
  muddy glory.

3 The puddings can be stored
  in the fridge for up to 4 days.
  The meringues should be stored
  separately in an airtight container
  at room temperature and placed on
  the puddings just before serving.

JANUSZ SAYS

*Aquafaba is the liquid left
over from cooking chickpeas,
or the liquid from a tin of
chickpeas.*

A buttery biscuit base with a rainbow-coloured sweet vanilla cheesecake filling, topped with a subtle lemon whipped cream. It's easy to bake and even easier to eat!

RAINBOW CHEESECAKE

BISCUIT BASE

120g (4¼oz) digestive (sweet wholemeal) biscuits
50g (1¾oz) unsalted butter, melted and cooled

CHEESECAKE FILLING

500g (1lb 2oz) cream cheese, room temperature
250g (9oz) mascarpone
3 large eggs, room temperature
400g (14oz) condensed milk
1 tablespoon natural vanilla extract
1 teaspoon cornflour (cornstarch)
¼ teaspoon each of red, orange, yellow, green, blue and purple gel food colouring

LEMON CREAM

300g (10½oz) double (thick) cream, chilled
40g (1½oz) icing (confectioners') sugar, sifted
1 tablespoon lemon zest

1 Preheat the oven to 170°C (325°F). Grease a 20cm (8 inch) springform cake tin and line the base with baking paper.

2 For the biscuit base, crush the digestive biscuits in a food processor until they are a sand-like consistency. Stir in the melted butter and mix until combined.

3 Add the biscuit mixture to the cake tin, firmly pressing it into the base, making sure it's evenly distributed. Place in the fridge.

4 For the cheesecake filling, in a mixing bowl, whip the cream cheese, mascarpone, eggs, condensed milk, vanilla and cornflour until smooth.

5 Divide the mixture evenly among six bowls. Add a different food colouring to each bowl and mix until well combined and the colours are even.

6 Remove the chilled base from the fridge. In the order of the rainbow, pour the coloured mixtures, one at a time, into the tin, starting with one colour in the very centre, and adding each colour in a circle around the preceding colour.

7 Place the tin into a larger roasting tin and pour in boiling water to reach halfway up the side of the cake tin. Bake for 60 minutes until the top of the cake is set but soft to the touch.

8 Turn the oven off and, with the oven door ajar, leave to cool for 2 hours.

9 Remove from the oven, then refrigerate for 4 hours.

10 For the lemon cream, in a stand mixer with the whisk attachment, whisk the chilled cream until stiff peaks form. Add the sugar and lemon zest and continue to whisk until fully combined.

11 Spread the whipped cream on top of the chilled cheesecake.

12 Refrigerate for 1 hour before removing from the tin and serving.

13 Store in the fridge for up to 3 days.

These honeybee-themed cupcakes are designed to remind you to simply Bee Yourself. The caramel sponge cupcakes are covered with chocolate honeycomb buttercream and topped with decorative homemade chocolate honeycomb shards. So take a bite and remember that YOU are a queen bee!

BEE YOURSELF CUPCAKES

CARAMEL CUPCAKES

120g (4¼oz) caster (superfine) sugar
25ml (¾fl oz) water
80g (2¾oz) unsalted butter, room temperature
1 egg, room temperature
1 teaspoon vanilla bean paste
100g (3½oz) plain (all-purpose) flour
½ teaspoon baking powder
½ teaspoon bicarbonate of soda (baking soda)
100ml (3½fl oz) buttermilk

1 Line a baking tray with baking paper.

2 Combine 70g (2½oz) of the sugar and the water in a small saucepan over high heat and cook until the mixture becomes a deep amber colour.

3 Pour the hot caramel onto the baking tray and leave to cool completely.

4 Once cool, transfer the caramel to a food processor and grind it into a powder.

5 Preheat the oven to 175°C (345°F). Line six holes of a muffin tin with paper cases.

6 In a mixing bowl, using hand-held electric beaters, beat the butter, then gradually add the caramel powder, a tablespoon at a time, followed by the remaining sugar, until fully incorporated. Add the egg and vanilla and mix until combined.

7 Sift half the flour, baking powder and bicarbonate of soda over the batter and mix well to combine. Add half the buttermilk and mix until combined.

8 Repeat step 7 with the remaining flour mixture and buttermilk.

9 Divide the cupcake mixture evenly among the paper cases. Bake for 18 minutes, or until a toothpick inserted into the cakes comes out clean. Leave to cool in the tin.

CHOCOLATE HONEYCOMB BUTTERCREAM

150g (5½oz) unsalted butter, room temperature
140g (5oz) condensed milk
60g (2¼oz) honeycomb covered in chocolate, broken into pieces
1½ tablespoons full-cream (whole) milk

1 In a stand mixer with the paddle attachment, beat the butter until pale and creamy. While mixing, add the condensed milk and mix until combined.

2 Put the honeycomb-covered chocolate and milk in a food processor and blitz for 1 minute on high speed.

3 Add the chocolate mixture to the buttercream and mix until well combined.

CHOCOLATE HONEYCOMB DECORATION

50g (1¾oz) caramel-flavoured chocolate, chopped

1 Heat the chocolate in the microwave on High in 20-second bursts, stirring after each burst, until melted.

2 Use a teaspoon to transfer a dollop of chocolate onto a honeycomb pattern mould or a piece of clean bubble wrap. Spread the dollop out with the back of a spoon until it is roughly the size of the top of your cupcakes. Repeat to make five more.

3 Allow the chocolate to set, then peel it off the mould or bubble wrap.

TO ASSEMBLE

80g (2¾oz) caramel sauce

1 Cut a 4cm (1½ inch) wide and deep hole in the centre of each cupcake. Spread buttercream over the sides and bottom of the hole, then fill with caramel sauce.

2 Transfer the remaining buttercream to a piping bag with a star nozzle.

3 Pipe a rosette of buttercream on top of each cupcake, then top with a chocolate honeycomb disc.

4 Store in an airtight container in the fridge for up to 3 days. Serve at room temperature.

MAKES 20

These indulgent chocolate fudge biscuits are topped with skin tone-coloured fondant icing which when rolled creates a stretch mark-like effect. They should be shared with everyone as a reminder that ALL bodies are beautiful and that we should be proud of the skin we're in.

BODY CONFIDENCE BISCUITS

CHOCOLATE FUDGE BISCUITS

80g (2¾oz) unsalted butter
50g (1¾oz) fudge
20g (¾oz) dark chocolate (80% cocoa solids), chopped
50g (1¾oz) caster (superfine) sugar
135g (4¾oz) plain (all-purpose) flour, sifted
¼ teaspoon baking powder, sifted

1. Grease a baking tray and line it with baking paper.

2. Combine the butter and fudge in a medium saucepan over medium heat, and stir with a whisk until melted.

3. Remove the pan from the heat. Add the chocolate and leave for 2 minutes, then stir until the chocolate is melted and the mixture is smooth.

4. Transfer the mixture to the bowl of a stand mixer and allow it to cool and solidify.

5. Use the stand mixer with the paddle attachment to mix until light and fluffy. Add the sugar and continue mixing for 1 minute. Add the remaining ingredients and mix until fully combined into a soft dough.

6. Wrap the dough in plastic wrap and refrigerate for 30 minutes – do not refrigerate for any longer or the mixture will become crumbly and difficult to work with.

7. Remove the dough from the fridge. On a floured work surface, roll out the dough until 5mm (¼ inch) thick.

8. Using a 7cm (2¾ inch) round cookie cutter, cut out 20 circles. Place the cookies on the baking tray and place in the freezer for 15 minutes.

9. Preheat the oven to 180°C (350°F).

10. Remove the tray from the freezer and bake for 10 minutes. Cool for 5 minutes on the tray, then transfer to a wire rack to cool completely.

TO ASSEMBLE

250g (9oz) fondant icing – in any skin colour from pale pink to chocolate!

1. Preheat the oven to 100°C (200°F). Grease a baking tray and line it with baking paper.

2. Divide the fondant icing in half and roll into two balls.

3. On a floured work surface, roll out one ball until about 5mm (¼ inch) thick.

4. Place the disc on the baking tray and bake for 5 minutes. Remove from the oven and cool to room temperature on the tray.

5. Roll out the second fondant icing ball until about 5mm (¼ inch) thick.

6. Place the baked fondant icing disc on top of the newly rolled one, then roll them out until about 2mm (1/16 inch) thick – you should see cracks appearing as you roll.

7. Using a 7cm (2¾ inch) round cookie cutter, cut out 20 circles from the fondant icing disc, then stick one on each of the biscuits, using a little water to secure them.

8. Once the fondant icing is dried on top of each biscuit, store in an airtight container for up to 1 week.

Nothing in life brings me as much pride and joy as being a dog dad to my sausage dog, Nigel, so it's only fair he made it into this book. Although cutting it feels wrong, this chocolate and cherry-flavoured sausage dog roulade is light and delicious and will bring you as much joy as Nigel brings to everyone he meets!

SAUSAGE DOG ROULADE

CHERRY CREAM
3 platinum gelatine leaves
100ml (3½fl oz) water
200g (7oz) frozen morello cherries
80g (2¾oz) caster (superfine) sugar
125g (4½oz) mascarpone
125g (4½oz) double (thick) cream

1   Soak the gelatine in the water.

2   Combine the cherries and sugar in a medium saucepan over high heat and cook for 5 minutes. Remove from the heat and blend to a purée using a hand-held blender.

3   Squeeze the excess water from the gelatine and add the gelatine to the hot fruit purée, mixing until the gelatine is dissolved. Set aside to cool.

4   In a stand mixer with the whisk attachment, whisk the mascarpone until light and fluffy. Add the cream and whisk until soft peaks form.

5   Add the cherry mixture to the mascarpone mixture and mix until combined – do not overwhip the mixture or it will not set.

6   Refrigerate for at least 2 hours.

CHERRY FILLING
100g (3½oz) frozen morello cherries
30g (1oz) caster (superfine) sugar
1 tablespoon lemon juice

1   Combine all the ingredients in a medium saucepan over high heat and cook, stirring occasionally, until most of the liquid has evaporated. Set aside to cool.

CHOCOLATE ROULADE

3 large eggs, room temperature, separated
100g (3½oz) caster (superfine) sugar
1 teaspoon vanilla bean paste
¼ teaspoon black gel food colouring
75g (2½oz) plain (all-purpose) flour
25g (1oz) pure unsweetened cocoa powder, plus extra to dust
½ teaspoon baking powder
50g (1¾oz) dark chocolate (70% cocoa solids), grated
icing (confectioners') sugar, sifted, to dust

1 Preheat the oven to 180°C (350°F). Line a 35 x 24cm (14 x 9½ inch) baking tin with baking paper.

2 In a stand mixer with the whisk attachment, whisk the egg whites until stiff peaks form. While whisking, gradually add the caster sugar, a tablespoon at a time, until fully incorporated.

3 In a separate bowl, briefly whisk the egg yolks with the vanilla and food colouring. Add this mixture to the meringue mixture and fold it in using a spatula until fully combined.

4 Mix the flour, cocoa and baking powder in a separate bowl. Sift half the flour mixture over the wet mixture, folding it in. Repeat with the remaining flour, cocoa and baking powder.

5 Add the grated chocolate and fold it in.

6 Transfer the mixture to the baking tin and level the surface.

7 Bake for 10 minutes until the sponge springs back when pressed with a finger.

8 Dust a clean tea towel (dish towel) with the extra cocoa and the icing sugar.

9 Remove the hot cake from the oven and invert it onto the dusted tea towel. Gently peel off the baking paper.

10 While still warm, starting from a short end, roll up the sponge inside the tea towel. Set aside to cool.

TO ASSEMBLE

250g (9oz) black fondant icing
20g (¾oz) brown fondant icing
20g (¾oz) white fondant icing
50g (1¾oz) red fondant icing
black gel food colouring

1 Carefully unroll the roulade from the tea towel.

2 Spread an even layer of the cherry cream over the top of the roulade, leaving a 2.5cm (1 inch) border at one short end.

3 Along the opposite short end, place the cherry filling in a line.

4 Starting from the short end with the cherry filling, roll up the roulade firmly. Place the roulade on a serving plate with the seam facing down.

5 Here's where we get less technical and more creative! Knead the black fondant icing for a couple of minutes until it's loosened and easy to roll.

6 Form a sausage dog-shaped head by making a large ball slightly bigger than the roulade. Start pulling out and flattening one side of the ball to form the snout.

7 Form the nose and ears (and eyebrows, if you want) out of the black fondant icing, and secure them in place with a little water.

8 Knead the brown fondant icing until it's loosened and easy to roll.

9 Use the brown fondant icing to create the brown sides of the dog's face.

10 Use the white and black fondant icings to create those cute puppy dog eyes. (Use the photo as a reference, or create your own design.)

11 Scrunch up some foil to form the shape of a dog's tail, then cover it with black fondant icing. Insert the tail into the roulade.

12 Knead and roll out the red fondant into a long strip. Cut a 1.5cm (⅝ inch) wide strip to create a collar. Place the collar onto the cake and stick the ends together with a very small amount of water.

13 Draw whiskers using a toothpick dipped in the black food colouring.

14 The roulade without the fondant icing decoration can be stored in the fridge for 48 hours. Once the decoration is added, the roulade should be served within a couple of hours.

SERVES 6

This dark and dreamy cake is flavoured with ube, a purple sweet potato with a nutty and strong vanilla taste. A bright purple sponge is covered in navy blue and purple buttercream to resemble a night sky decorated with a constellation in the shape of your or your loved one's star sign. This makes a fabulous birthday cake and is perfect for the moment you make that special birthday wish.

ZODIAC CAKE

PURPLE UBE SPONGE

3 large eggs, room temperature, separated
100g (3½oz) caster (superfine) sugar
60ml (2fl oz) vegetable oil
2 teaspoons ube extract
¼ teaspoon purple gel food colouring
100g (3½oz) ube jam
¼ teaspoon cream of tartar
120g (4¼oz) plain (all-purpose) flour
1 teaspoon baking powder

1   Preheat the oven to 180°C (350°F). Line the base of a 20cm (8 inch) round springform cake tin with baking paper.

2   In a large mixing bowl, whisk the egg yolks and 30g (1oz) of the sugar until light and fluffy. Add the oil, ube extract and food colouring and mix until well combined. Add the ube jam and mix until well combined.

3   In a stand mixer with the whisk attachment, whisk the egg whites until slightly foamy. Add the cream of tartar and whisk until stiff peaks form.

4   While whisking on high speed, gradually add the remaining sugar, a tablespoon at a time, until fully incorporated.

5   Sift half the flour and baking powder over the egg yolk mixture and mix until combined.

6   Using a spatula, fold in one-third of the meringue mixture until combined.

7   Sift the remaining flour and baking powder over the mixture and fold them in until combined.

8   Add the remaining meringue mixture and fold it in until combined.

9   Pour the batter into the tin, level the surface, then bake for 40 minutes until a toothpick inserted into the cake comes out clean.

10   Remove from the oven and leave to cool in the tin for 5 minutes. Turn the cake tin upside down and let the cake cool completely before cutting it out of the tin using a sharp serrated knife. Transfer to a wire rack to cool completely.

11   Once cool, cut the cake in half vertically to create two semi-circles. Set aside.

PURPLE UBE BUTTERCREAM

3 large egg whites, room
   temperature
160g (5½oz) caster (superfine)
   sugar
250g (9oz) unsalted butter, room
   temperature, cubed
2 teaspoons ube extract
purple and navy gel food colouring

1   Place the egg whites and sugar in a glass or metal bowl sitting on top of a pan of simmering water, ensuring the water is not touching the base of the bowl. Whisk constantly until the mixture reaches 70°C (150°F) on a sugar thermometer.

2   Transfer to a stand mixer with the whisk attachment and whisk on a medium–high speed for 10 minutes.

3   Change to the paddle attachment and add the butter, a cube at a time. Whisk until smooth.

4   Reserve 2 tablespoons of the buttercream and set aside. Add the ube extract to the remaining buttercream and mix to combine.

5   Divide the mixture evenly between two bowls. Add three drops of purple food colouring to one bowl. To the second bowl add the navy blue food colouring, ¼ teaspoon at a time, until you achieve a deep navy blue. Mix until well combined and the colours are even.

TO ASSEMBLE

1   Use 3 tablespoons of the purple buttercream to sandwich both halves of the cake together – one on top of the other so you have a layered semicircle. Place on a cake board with the flat surface of the cake at the bottom. You now have an upright semicircular cake.

2   Spread the remaining purple buttercream all around the bottom half of the cake, then spread the navy blue buttercream over the rest of the surface – you are trying to achieve an ombré effect that looks like the night sky (see photograph).

3   Smooth the buttercream using a palette knife.

4   Use some of the reserved white buttercream and a palette knife to create cloud-like effects around the cake.

5   Transfer the remaining white buttercream to a piping bag with a very small plain nozzle and pipe your desired star sign constellation onto on the flat surfaces of the cake.

6   Join the stars up using piped dotted lines and, when complete, decorate the rest of the cake surface with small random white dots representing the night stars.

7   Store in the fridge for up to 4 days. Serve at room temperature.

JANUSZ SAYS

You can find ube extract and ube jam in Asian supermarkets.

MAKES 50

When I first moved to the UK, I had a job in a nursing home and it was there that I discovered the British obsession with biscuits. One of my favourite things to bake and gift to people is a batch of my homemade ginger biscuits. However, for this book, I have elevated my recipe by incorporating chocolate. The spiciness of the ginger works perfectly with the bittersweet chocolate.

CHOCOLATE GINGER BISCUITS

175g (6oz) salted butter, room temperature
120g (4¼oz) dark brown sugar
100g (3½oz) caster (superfine) sugar
1 tablespoon natural vanilla extract
1 tablespoon treacle
1 tablespoon honey
1 large egg, room temperature
300g (10½oz) plain (all-purpose) flour
3 tablespoons pure unsweetened cocoa powder
3 tablespoons ground ginger
1½ tablespoons ground cinnamon
½ teaspoon ground cloves
1 teaspoon bicarbonate of soda (baking soda)

1   Grease two baking trays and line them with baking paper.

2   In a stand mixer with the paddle attachment, beat the butter until pale and creamy. While mixing, gradually add the sugars, a tablespoon at a time, until fully incorporated. Add the vanilla, treacle and honey and mix until combined. Add the egg and mix until combined.

3   Sift the flour, cocoa, spices and bicarbonate of soda over the mixture and mix until combined.

4   Divide the dough into 15g (½oz) pieces and roll each one into a walnut-sized ball. Place on the baking trays and refrigerate for 30 minutes.

5   Preheat the oven to 180°C (350°F).

6   Once cool, flatten the top of the balls slightly and bake for 10 minutes.

7   Remove from the oven and leave to cool on the trays for 5 minutes. Transfer to a wire rack to cool completely.

8   Store in an airtight container for up to 7 days.

MAKES 12

This recipe is inspired by my favourite LGBTQ+ musical, *The Rocky Horror Picture Show*. Containing popping candy, red sweet lips, salted popcorn, marshmallows, dried sour cherries and ginger biscuits, this bake will surprise you and help you give in to absolute pleasure, with the smell alone making you shiver with antici ... pation!

ROCKY HORROR ROAD

125g (4½oz) unsalted butter

300g (10½oz) dark chocolate (50% cocoa solids), chopped

150g (5½oz) ginger nut biscuits (ginger snaps, or use my Chocolate Ginger Biscuits recipe on page 64), broken into large pieces

25g (1oz) jelly red lip candies

40g (1½oz) salted popcorn

40g (1½oz) dried sour cherries

30g (1oz) mini marshmallows

10g (⅓oz) popping candy

30g (1oz) white chocolate, chopped

⅛ teaspoon red gel food colouring

50g (1¾oz) edible pearls

1 Line a deep 20cm (8 inch) square baking tin with baking paper.

2 In a medium saucepan over medium heat, melt the butter and dark chocolate, stirring to combine. Set aside.

3 In a large bowl, place the ginger biscuits, jellies, popcorn, cherries, marshmallows and popping candy and mix to combine.

4 Pour two-thirds of the melted dark chocolate mixture into the bowl and mix until all the ingredients are evenly coated.

5 Transfer the mixture to the tin, pressing down firmly with a spatula to remove any air pockets.

6 Pour the remaining melted chocolate over the top.

7 Refrigerate for at least 1 hour until firm.

8 Heat the white chocolate in the microwave on High in 20-second bursts, stirring after each burst, until melted.

9 Add the red food colouring to the white chocolate and mix until combined and the colour is even.

10 Transfer the melted chocolate to a disposable piping bag with a very small hole cut at the tip. Pipe a criss-cross fish-net effect over the cold rocky road. Place an edible pearl in every cross-section of the fish-net (see photograph).

11 Return the tin to the fridge for at least 30 minutes.

12 Cut the rocky road into 12 portions. Store in an airtight container in the fridge for up to 1 week. Serve at room temperature.

SERVES 8

One of the best things about baking is how it encourages creativity. I made this apple sponge and spiced apple buttercream art-themed drip cake to remind everyone that – no matter your level of baking skills – you should have fun in the kitchen and be proud of whatever you create!

ARTISTIC DRIP CAKE

APPLE SPONGE

4 orange-red apples, peeled, cored and cut into 1.5cm (⅝ inch) pieces
juice of ½ lemon
125g (4½oz) unsalted butter, room temperature
100g (3½oz) soft brown sugar
3 large eggs, room temperature, separated
1 teaspoon vanilla bean paste
175g (6oz) plain (all-purpose) flour
2 teaspoons baking powder

1 Preheat the oven to 180°C (350°F). Grease three 15cm (6 inch) round cake tins and line the bases with baking paper.

2 In a large mixing bowl, combine the apple pieces and lemon juice and mix well to ensure all the apple is covered in lemon juice. Set aside.

3 In a stand mixer with the paddle attachment, beat the butter until pale and creamy. While mixing, gradually add the sugar, a tablespoon at a time, until fully incorporated. Add the egg yolks and vanilla and mix until combined.

4 Sift the flour and baking powder over the mixture and use a spatula to mix until combined.

5 Add the apple pieces to the batter and mix well.

6 In a large mixing bowl, whisk the egg whites until stiff peaks form.

7 Gently fold the beaten egg whites into the cake batter using a spatula.

8 Distribute the batter evenly between the three tins.

9 Bake for 30 minutes until a toothpick inserted into the cakes comes out clean. Set aside to cool in the tins.

SPICED APPLE BUTTERCREAM FILLING

1 orange-red apple, peeled, cored and grated
2 tablespoons ground cinnamon
1 teaspoon ground ginger
¼ teaspoon ground cloves
¼ teaspoon ground nutmeg
70g (2½oz) soft brown sugar
150g (5½oz) unsalted butter, room temperature
150g (5½oz) icing (confectioners') sugar

1 In a medium saucepan over medium–high heat, combine the grated apple, spices and sugar and cook until the mixture thickens and forms a stiff purée. Set aside to cool.

2 In a stand mixer with the paddle attachment, beat the butter until pale and creamy. While beating, gradually add the sugar, a tablespoon at a time, until fully incorporated. Add the apple purée and mix until fully combined.

WHITE VANILLA BUTTERCREAM

150g (5½oz) unsalted butter, room
  temperature
150g (5½oz) condensed milk
1 teaspoon vanilla bean paste

1 In a stand mixer with the paddle
   attachment, beat the butter until pale
   and creamy. Add the condensed milk
   and mix until fully combined. Add
   the vanilla and mix on a low speed to
   remove any large air bubbles.

2 Reserve 6 teaspoons of the
   buttercream for later use and
   transfer the remaining buttercream
   to a piping bag with a plain nozzle.

RAINBOW DRIP

2 tablespoons double (thick) cream
100g (3½oz) white chocolate,
  chopped
⅛ teaspoon each of red, orange,
  yellow, green, blue and purple gel
  food colouring

1 Heat the cream in the microwave
   on High for 30 seconds.

2 Add the white chocolate and
   return the bowl to the microwave for
   30 seconds. Stir until fully combined.

3 Divide the chocolate mixture evenly
   among six bowls. Add a different
   food colouring to each bowl and mix
   until well combined and the colours
   are even.

TO ASSEMBLE

50g (1¾oz) caramel-flavoured
  chocolate, chopped
5 long pretzel sticks
  (12–15cm/4½–6 inches)
⅛ teaspoon each of red, orange,
  yellow, green, blue and purple gel
  food colouring

1 Place one of the sponges in the
   centre of a cake board or serving
   plate and top with one-quarter of
   the apple buttercream.

2 Place the second sponge on top and
   spread with another one-quarter of
   the apple buttercream.

3 Place the last sponge on top, smooth
   side facing up, and use the remaining
   apple buttercream to coat the top of
   the cake with a smooth finish.

4 Cover the top and side of the cake
   with the white vanilla buttercream
   and smooth using a cake scraper
   or palette knife.

5 Refrigerate for 30 minutes.

6 While the cake is cooling, heat the
   caramel chocolate in a small glass in
   the microwave on High in 20-second
   bursts, stirring after each burst, until
   melted.

7 Dip the pretzel sticks into the melted
   caramel chocolate and leave to set
   on a sheet of baking paper.

8 Spread out the remaining caramel
   chocolate on a sheet of baking
   paper.

9 When the chocolate begins to
   set, use a knife to cut out the shape
   of a painter's palette about 10cm
   (4 inches) wide.

10 When fully set, carefully remove the
    chocolate palette from the paper
    and set aside.

11 You are going to decorate two-thirds
    of the top of the cake with the drip,
    while leaving one-third plain where
    you will place the palette later. Start
    each colour in the middle of the
    cake, then create a wedge of each
    colour and finish with a few drips of
    the colour spilling down the side of
    the cake.

12 Colour 1 teaspoon of the reserved
    white buttercream with each of the
    same six colours as the drips.

13 Using a piping bag with a plain
    nozzle, pipe a blob of each coloured
    buttercream into the centre of the
    cake, then brush it with a pastry
    brush to add texture. These blobs
    will be the 'brush' part of your
    paintbrushes. Insert a chocolate-
    covered pretzel into each blob of
    buttercream to create the paintbrush
    handles. Lean the paintbrushes at
    an angle.

14 Finally, place the chocolate paint
    palette on top of the third of the cake
    that you left plain. Add a tiny amount
    of each coloured buttercream to
    resemble blobs of paint on the
    palette.

15 Store in the fridge for up to 3 days.
    Serve at room temperature.

If there's one thing I appreciate more than life itself, it's the ability to capture the very best moments on film to look back on. I love taking photos wherever I go, so I wanted to share this recipe for a fun iced sugar biscuit for you to use to frame and caption the special occasions in your life. There are even some companies who will print your photos on edible paper.

EDIBLE PHOTO FRAME BISCUITS

SUGAR BISCUITS

100g (3½oz) unsalted butter, room temperature
90g (3¼oz) soft light brown sugar
1 large egg yolk, room temperature
2 tablespoons maple syrup
½ teaspoon vanilla bean paste
150g (5½oz) plain (all-purpose) flour

1   Grease two baking trays and line them with baking paper.

2   In a stand mixer with the paddle attachment, beat the butter until pale and creamy. While mixing, add the sugar, a tablespoon at a time, until fully incorporated. Add the egg yolk, maple syrup and vanilla and mix until combined.

3   Sift the flour over the mixture and mix until a soft dough is formed.

4   Wrap the dough in plastic wrap and refrigerate for 30 minutes.

5   Remove the dough from the fridge and let it rest for 10 minutes.

6   On a floured work surface, roll out the dough until 7mm (⅜ inch) thick.

7   Using a 10 x 6cm (4 x 2½ inch) cookie cutter, cut out 12 rectangles.

8   Place the rectangles on the baking trays and cut a smaller rectangular hole in the dough, so they resemble picture frames. Freeze the dough for 15 minutes. (You can use the dough scraps to make Pride flag biscuits.)

9   Preheat the oven to 180°C (350°F).

10 Remove from the freezer and bake for 9 minutes, or until slightly golden. Leave to cool on the tray for 5 minutes, then transfer to a wire rack to cool completely.

LEMON ICING

1 large pasteurised egg white (pasteurised egg whites in cartons are sold at most supermarkets), room temperature
200g (7oz) icing (confectioners') sugar, sifted
2 tablespoons lemon juice

1   In a stand mixer with the whisk attachment, whisk the egg white until stiff peaks form. While whisking, gradually add the icing sugar, a tablespoon at a time, until fully incorporated. Stir in the lemon juice.

2   Transfer the icing to a piping bag with a small plain nozzle.

TO ASSEMBLE

black edible food marker pens

1   Pipe icing over your biscuit frames to resemble white Instax frames.

2   Leave until the icing has set hard before serving. Provide your guests with edible food marker pens so that messages can be written on the biscuits, which can then be used as fun, tasty frames for real-life photos.

3   Store in an airtight container for up to 7 days.

MAKES 6

These rainbow cupcakes are a fun and colourful twist on classic cupcakes and are perfect for a party. The fluffy lemon cupcake base is topped with vibrant rainbow swirls of buttercream and then finished with a cherry on top.

RAINBOW CHERRY CUPCAKES

LEMON CUPCAKES

90g (3¼oz) unsalted butter, room temperature
60g (2¼oz) caster (superfine) sugar
1 large egg, room temperature
1 teaspoon vanilla bean paste
1 teaspoon lemon zest
90g (3¼oz) plain (all-purpose) flour
¾ teaspoon baking powder

1 Preheat the oven to 180°C (350°F). Line six holes of a muffin tin with paper cases.

2 In a stand mixer with the paddle attachment, beat the butter until pale and creamy. While mixing, add the sugar, a tablespoon at a time, until fully incorporated. Add the egg, vanilla and lemon zest and mix until combined.

3 Sift the flour and baking powder over the mixture and fold them in using a spatula.

4 Transfer the batter into the cases in the tray and bake for 18 minutes until golden on top and a toothpick inserted into the cupcakes comes out clean.

RAINBOW BUTTERCREAM

300g (10½oz) unsalted butter, room temperature
300g (10½oz) condensed milk
1 tablespoon lemon zest
¼ teaspoon each of orange, yellow, green, blue and purple gel food colouring

1 In a stand mixer with the paddle attachment, beat the butter until pale and creamy. Add the condensed milk and lemon zest and mix until combined.

2 Divide the mixture into five bowls, but decrease the amount of buttercream in each bowl. The bowl with the most buttercream (purple) will be the bottom layer and the one with the least (orange) will be the top.

3 Add a different food colouring to each bowl and mix until well combined and the colours are even.

4 Transfer the buttercreams to five separate piping bags with plain nozzles.

TO ASSEMBLE

6 glacé cherries with stems attached

1 Using one colour at a time, starting with the piping bag with the most buttercream (purple), pipe concentric circles of buttercream, one on top of the other, to create a rainbow topping (see photograph).

2 Top each cupcake with a cherry.

3 Store in the fridge for up to 3 days. Serve at room temperature.

MAKES 5

You'll *bear-ly* believe how easy it is to make these tasty sweet buns filled with baked strawberries and topped with a cookie crumble. They were a childhood favourite of mine, so they're a recipe close to my heart.

STRAWBERRY—FILLED BEAR BUNS

BEAR BUNS

220g (7¾oz) strong flour
7g (¼oz) active dried yeast
2 tablespoons caster (superfine) sugar
⅛ teaspoon salt
110ml (3½fl oz) full-cream (whole) milk, warm
2 large egg yolks, room temperature, plus 1 beaten egg
1½ tablespoons vegetable oil
brown gel food colouring

STRAWBERRY FILLING

2½ teaspoons almond meal
15 large fresh strawberries, sliced

COOKIE CRUST TOPPING

40g (1½oz) plain (all-purpose) flour
3 tablespoons sugar
30g (1oz) unsalted butter, melted
½ teaspoon natural vanilla extract

1   For the bear buns, in a stand mixer with the dough hook attachment, mix the flour, yeast, sugar, salt, milk and egg yolks on medium speed for 7 minutes. Add the oil and mix for a further 5 minutes until the dough starts to come away from the side of the bowl.

2   Cover the bowl with plastic wrap and leave to prove in a warm place for 90 minutes.

3   Punch the dough down, knead it briefly on a floured work surface, then divide it into five equal portions.

4   From each portion remove two 1cm (½ inch) balls of dough and one 5mm (¼ inch) ball.

5   Roll the five portions of dough into balls and flatten them slightly.

6   To each large flattened ball, add two 1cm (½ inch) balls to the sides to resemble ears. Flatten the 5mm (¼ inch) balls and stick them on the top of each large ball to resemble a bear's nose.

7   Set aside, cover with a tea towel (dish towel) and leave to prove in a warm place for 40 minutes.

8   Preheat the oven to 175°C (345°F).

9   Press the oiled bottom of a glass into the dough, slightly off-centre (closer to the bottom so the bear's face is untouched).

10 Fill the indent with ½ teaspoon of almond meal and three or four strawberry slices.

11 Mix all the ingredients for the cookie crust topping together in a bowl.

12 Cover the strawberries on each bear's face with one-fifth of the cookie crumb mixture.

13 Brush the dough with beaten egg and leave to stand for 5 minutes.

14 Bake for 17 minutes until brown.

15 Once baked and cooled, use a toothpick dipped in the brown food colouring to draw a cute bear nose and eyes.

16 These are best eaten on the day they are made.

MAKES 14

Like baking, I use fashion to express my identity and creativity. I am often complimented on my bold, colourful jumpers and firmly believe that, when it comes to fashion, there are no rules. Have fun with your friends decorating these pistachio-flavoured sweater-shaped cookies. Use an assortment of coloured icing and decorations and release your inner fashion designer.

FASHIONISTA COOKIES

PISTACHIO COOKIES
60g (2¼oz) pistachios
100g (3½oz) unsalted butter, cold, cubed
60g (2¼oz) caster (superfine) sugar
120g (4¼oz) plain (all-purpose) flour, sifted
1 teaspoon vanilla bean paste
pinch of salt

1 Preheat the oven to 175°C (345°F). Grease three baking trays and line them with baking paper.

2 Spread the pistachios on one tray and bake for 10 minutes, shaking once after 5 minutes.

3 Allow the pistachios to cool, then blitz them in a food processor for about 20 seconds until they form a powder with some small visible pieces of pistachio.

4 In a stand mixer with the paddle attachment, mix the pistachio powder with the remaining ingredients until a stiff dough forms.

5 Wrap the dough in plastic wrap and refrigerate for 30 minutes.

6 Remove the dough from the fridge and let it rest for 10 minutes.

7 On a floured work surface, roll out the dough to about 5mm (¼ inch) thick. Using a 10cm (4 inch) sweater-shaped cookie cutter (or a knife and a template made from card), cut out 14 cookies.

8 Preheat the oven to 180°C (350°F).

9 Place on the baking trays and freeze for 15 minutes.

10 Remove from the freezer and bake for 10 minutes – the edges of the cookies should be golden. Remove from the oven and cool slightly on the trays, then transfer to a wire rack to cool completely.

TO ASSEMBLE
1 large pasteurised egg white (pasteurised egg whites in cartons are sold at most supermarkets), room temperature
200g (7oz) icing (confectioners') sugar, sifted
1 teaspoon lemon juice
selection of gel food colourings
assorted edible cake decorations

1 Whisk the egg white until stiff peaks form. While whisking, gradually add the sugar, a tablespoon at a time, until fully incorporated. Add the lemon juice and mix to combine.

2 Divide the mixture evenly among five bowls and add three drops of a different food colouring to each bowl. Mix until well combined and the colours are even.

3 Transfer the mixture to five separate piping bags with small plain piping nozzles.

4 Serve along with an assortment of edible decorations and let your fashionista guests decorate their own cookies with the icing and decorations.

5 Store in an airtight container for up to 7 days.

MAKES 7

As somebody who embraces body positivity and loves to see others appreciate their own attributes, I wanted to share this peach mochi recipe that I created to celebrate my peachy derrière! These mochi have a soft, squidgy exterior shaped like the iconic peach emoji, and a delicious peach-flavoured cream.

PEACH MOCHI

MOCHI
60g (2¼oz) cornflour (cornstarch)
125g (4½oz) sweet glutinous rice flour
35g (1¼oz) caster (superfine) sugar
80ml (2½fl oz) water
185ml (6fl oz) peach juice
1 drop of peach or coral gel food colouring

1 Toast the cornflour in a frying pan over medium–high heat for 1 minute. Remove from the heat and set aside.

2 In a microwave-safe bowl, combine the rice flour, sugar, water, juice and food colouring. Mix well, then heat in the microwave on High for 2 minutes. Remove from the microwave, dip a spatula in cold water and stir the mixture. Microwave for a further 2 minutes and stir again.

3 Dust a work surface with the toasted cornflour (put most of it in the middle where the mochi will be).

4 Transfer the mochi mixture to the centre of the work surface and leave to cool for 5 minutes.

5 Rub the cornflour over the top and sides of the mochi.

6 Roll the mochi into a 25 x 7.5cm (10 x 3 inch) rectangle. Leave to cool for a further 5 minutes.

7 Pinch off golf ball-sized portions of mochi and roll them into balls. Roll the balls in cornflour and set aside.

PEACH FILLING
1 platinum gelatine leaf
100ml (3½fl oz) water
200g (7oz) fresh peaches, finely chopped
50g (1¾oz) caster (superfine) sugar
1 tablespoon lemon juice
60g (2¼oz) cream cheese, room temperature
100g (3½oz) double (thick) cream

1 Soak the gelatine in the water.

2 Place the chopped peaches, sugar and lemon juice in a saucepan over medium–high heat and cook for about 5 minutes until the fruit is soft and the mixture has thickened. Remove the pan from the heat.

3 Squeeze the excess water from the gelatine and add the gelatine to the hot peach mixture. Mix well to combine. Allow the peach mixture to cool, but make sure it doesn't set.

4 In a bowl using hand-held electric beaters, whip the cream cheese to loosen it. Add the cream and whip until soft peaks form.

5 Fold the cream mixture into the peach mixture using a spatula and refrigerate for at least 2 hours.

TO ASSEMBLE

1 Flatten each ball into a disc about 2cm (¾ inch) thick.

2 Add 1 teaspoon of peach filling to the centre of each disc. Fold the mochi around the filling and pinch to seal. Roll into balls again.

3 Use a butter knife to make a line in the top of each ball so they look like peaches.

4 Place each ball in a paper case and store them in the fridge for up to 3 days.

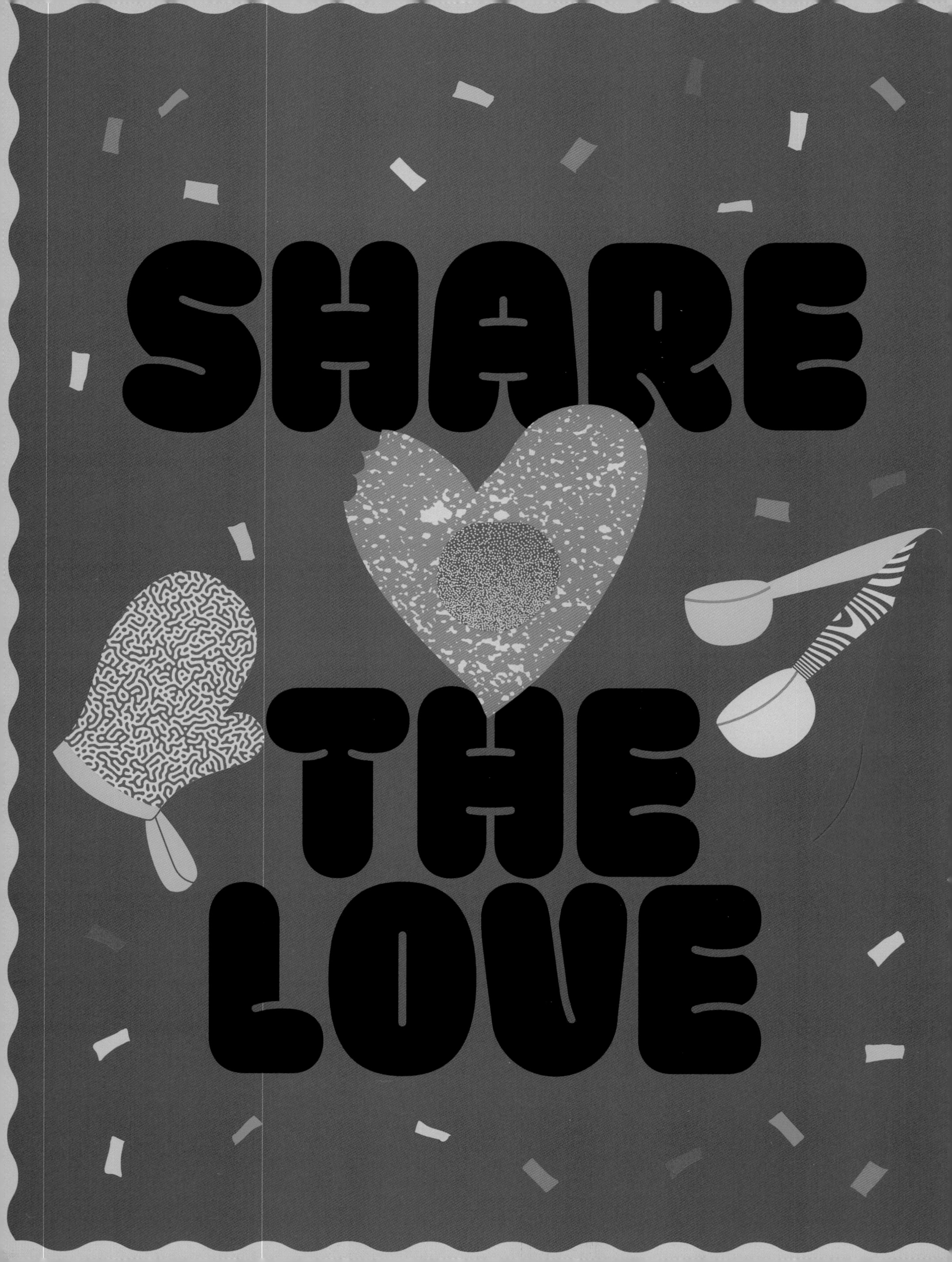
SHARE
THE
LOVE

While I've been known to slide into DMs, I'm an old romantic at heart and enjoy writing love letters. These sweet, three-layer, rose and honey-flavoured biscuits have a space inside them to conceal a handwritten note for your loved one.

LOVE LETTER BISCUITS

ROSE & HONEY BISCUITS

100g (3½oz) unsalted butter, room temperature
75g (2½oz) creamed honey
160g (5½oz) plain (all-purpose) flour
20g (¾oz) cornflour (cornstarch)
30g (1oz) icing (confectioners') sugar, sifted
1 teaspoon rose water

1 Combine all the ingredients in a stand mixer with the paddle attachment and mix until combined and a soft dough forms.

2 Wrap the dough in plastic wrap and refrigerate for 30 minutes.

3 Preheat the oven to 180°C (350°F). Grease two baking trays and line them with baking paper.

4 Remove the dough from the fridge and let it rest for 10 minutes.

5 On a floured work surface, roll the dough out until 5mm (¼ inch) thick.

6 Using a 9 x 6cm (3½ x 2½ inch) rectangular cookie cutter (or a knife and a template made from card), cut out 12 rectangles.

7 Using a smaller rectangular cookie cutter, cut a hole inside four of the biscuits, leaving just a 6 x 3cm (2½ x 1¼ inch) frame of dough – this will create the cavity to hold the love letter. (You can bake the cut-out rectangles separately if you like as extra sweet treats.)

8 Place eight whole biscuits and the four cut-out biscuits on two baking trays and freeze for 10 minutes.

9 Remove from the freezer and bake the biscuits for 10 minutes until the edges are golden. Leave to cool on the trays for a few minutes, then transfer to a wire rack to cool completely.

LEMON ICING

5g (⅛oz) egg white powder
1½ tablespoons water
170g (6oz) icing (confectioners') sugar, sifted
1 tablespoon lemon juice

1 Combine the egg white powder and water and set aside for 20 minutes.

2 Strain the mixture into a bowl.

3 Add half the sugar to the strained liquid and mix to combine. Add the remaining sugar and stir until fully incorporated. Stir in the lemon juice until combined.

4 Transfer one-third of the icing to a piping bag with a very small plain nozzle.

TO ASSEMBLE

4 love letters written on A6
  (15 x 10.5cm/6 x 4 inch) paper
¼ teaspoon red gel food colouring

1. Place four whole biscuits on a work surface and apply a layer of icing around the edge. Apply a second layer of icing to the underside of one of the frame-shaped biscuits and stick the two biscuits (icing to icing) together.

2. Fold a handwritten love letter and place it inside the gap left by the biscuit frame.

3. Apply a layer of icing around the surface of the frame-shaped biscuit and also the edge of another whole biscuit and stick them together, sealing the note inside. Now you have a three-tiered biscuit, pipe a neat border of icing around the edge of the top biscuit, flood the centre with icing and smooth the surface. Pipe lines to indicate the folds in the envelope (see photograph).

4. Once dry, add the red food colouring to the remaining icing.

5. Pipe a love heart in the centre of the biscuit (see photograph). Allow to dry, then deliver with love.

6. Store in an airtight container at room temperature for up to 5 days.

Although they should, not all kings and queens wear crowns. Celebrate the kings and queens in your life with these delicious shortbread sandwich tarts filled with homemade strawberry jam and a light vanilla cream.

KING/QUEEN OF TARTS

SHORTBREAD PASTRY

160g (5½oz) unsalted butter, cold, cubed
230g (8½oz) plain (all-purpose) flour, sifted
80g (2¾oz) caster (superfine) sugar
1½ tablespoons sour cream
2 large egg yolks, room temperature
1 teaspoon vanilla bean paste

1 Grease two baking trays and line them with baking paper.

2 In a stand mixer with the paddle attachment, mix the butter, flour and sugar on low speed until the texture resembles breadcrumbs.

3 Add the sour cream, egg yolks and vanilla and mix until a soft dough forms.

4 Wrap the dough in plastic wrap and refrigerate for 1 hour.

5 Remove the dough from the fridge and let it rest for 10 minutes.

6 On a floured work surface, roll out the dough until 5mm (¼ inch) thick.

7 Using a 9 x 6cm (3½ x 2½ inch) rectangular cookie cutter (or a knife and a template made from card), cut out 20 rectangles.

8 In half of the rectangles, cut out two small hearts in the top left and bottom right hand corners and the letters Q or K in the centre, resembling playing cards. (You can buy small alphabet cookie cutters online. However, if you cannot find them, use a small sharp knife or scalpel to cut out the shapes.)

9 Place the biscuits on the baking trays and put them in the freezer for 20 minutes. Preheat the oven to 180°C (350°F).

10 Remove the biscuits from the freezer and bake for 12 minutes or until the edges are golden. Cool for a few minutes on the trays, then transfer to a wire rack to cool completely.

STRAWBERRY JAM

200g (7oz) strawberries
220g (7¾oz) jam sugar
juice of 1 large lemon

1 In a medium saucepan, mash the strawberries. Add the remaining ingredients and stir well.

2 Place the pan over high heat and stir until boiling. Cook for 4 minutes, then remove from the heat and set aside to cool.

WHIPPED VANILLA CREAM

2 platinum gelatine leaves
100ml (3½fl oz) water
250g (9oz) double (thick) cream
30g (1oz) icing (confectioners')
    sugar, sifted
1 teaspoon vanilla bean paste

1   Soak the gelatine in the water for
    10 minutes. Squeeze out any excess
    water, then melt the gelatine in the
    microwave on High for 5 seconds.
    Set aside.

2   In a stand mixer with the whisk
    attachment, whip the cream, sugar
    and vanilla until soft peaks form.
    Add the gelatine and whisk until
    combined and the mixture
    has thickened.

3   Transfer the cream to a piping bag
    with a star nozzle.

TO ASSEMBLE

2 tablespoons icing
    (confectioners') sugar

1   Place one biscuit on a plate. Pipe a
    border of the cream filling around the
    edge, then spread a small amount in
    the middle.

2   Spoon the jam into the centre of
    the cream and top it with one of the
    king or queen 'playing card' biscuits,
    pressing down to ensure jam
    squeezes through the holes in the
    top card.

3   Place extra jam in each symbol
    hole if required, but use a syringe
    or a piping bag with a very small
    hole if possible to keep things neat.
    Dust the biscuits with icing sugar
    and serve.

4   Store in the fridge in an airtight
    container for up to 2 days. Keep
    in mind that the tarts will become
    softer – which is a desirable thing!

JANUSZ SAYS

*For convenience you could
use good-quality store-
bought jam. Simply give it a
quick whisk before spooning it
over the cream. Morello cherry
jam is also a good choice.*

Celebrate your sweet loves with these tear-and-share bear buns. The soft, airy, honey-flavoured, bear-shaped buns are filled with a honey cream and decorated with a cute chocolate face.

HONEY TEAR-&-SHARE BEAR BUNS

HONEY BUNS
500g (1lb 2oz) strong flour, sifted
10g (⅓oz) active dried yeast
260ml (9¼fl oz) full-cream (whole) milk, lukewarm
90g (3¼oz) runny honey
3 large egg yolks, room temperature
60g (2¼oz) unsalted butter, melted and cooled

HONEY CREAM FILLING
110g (3¾oz) unsalted butter
3 tablespoons plain (all-purpose) flour, sifted
180ml (5¾fl oz) evaporated milk
100g (3½oz) runny honey

DECORATION
25g (1oz) dark chocolate (70% cocoa solids)
12 large white chocolate buttons

1. Grease and line a 35 x 24 x 5cm (14 x 9½ x 2 inch) baking tin with baking paper.

2. For the buns, in a stand mixer with the dough hook attachment, mix the flour, yeast, milk, honey and egg yolks for several minutes on medium speed. Add the melted butter and mix for a further 5 minutes until a dough forms.

3. Cover the bowl with plastic wrap and let it prove in a warm place for 90 minutes.

4. For the honey cream filling, heat the butter in a saucepan over medium heat. Once the butter is melted and bubbling, add the flour and mix to combine. While stirring, slowly pour in the evaporated milk. Add the honey and cook for 1 minute. Remove from the heat, cover with plastic wrap touching the surface, to prevent a skin forming, and set aside to cool.

5. Punch the dough down and knead it briefly on a floured work surface.

6. Divide the dough into 13 equal portions.

7. Flatten 12 portions of the dough with your hand and place 1½ tablespoons of filling in each. Seal the dough around the filling, then roll the dough into balls. Place the balls in the baking tin.

8. Use the remaining dough portion to make 12 sets of ears and attach them to the tops of the buns in the baking tin. Leave the buns to prove in a warm place for 30 minutes.

9. Preheat the oven to 180°C (350°F).

10. Bake the buns for 18 minutes until golden brown. Let the buns cool completely in the tin.

11. Heat the dark chocolate in the microwave on High in 15-second bursts, stirring between bursts, until melted.

12. Transfer the chocolate to a piping bag with a very small plain nozzle.

13. Use the dark chocolate to draw a nose and mouth on the white chocolate buttons. Attach the white button faces to the buns. Pipe two dots for eyes above the button.

14. The buns are best eaten on the day of making, but you can store leftovers in an airtight container for up to 24 hours.

SERVES 12

Nothing says romance quite like chocolate, strawberries and champagne, so treat your loved ones with this decadent white chocolate sponge cake. It's filled with a delicate strawberry and champagne-infused jelly and topped with a luscious white chocolate mousse.

STRAWBERRY & CHAMPAGNE CAKE

350g (12oz) white chocolate, chopped, plus 50g (1¾oz) extra, grated

60g (2¼oz) salted butter, room temperature

60g (2¼oz) caster (superfine) sugar

2 large eggs, room temperature, separated

1 teaspoon natural vanilla extract

60g (2¼oz) plain (all-purpose) flour

½ teaspoon baking powder

600g (1lb 5oz) fresh strawberries, plus 10 halved strawberries to garnish

1 packet strawberry jelly (gelatine dessert) powder (enough to set 600ml/21fl oz liquid)

50ml (1½fl oz) champagne or prosecco

150ml (5fl oz) full-cream (whole) milk

1 vanilla bean, split and seeds scraped

2 teaspoons gelatine powder

2 tablespoons cold water

250g (9oz) double (thick) cream

1   Preheat the oven to 170°C (325°F). Grease a 23cm (9 inch) round springform cake tin and line the base with baking paper.

2   Heat 50g (1¾oz) of the chopped white chocolate in the microwave on High in 15-second bursts, stirring after each burst, until melted. Set aside to cool.

3   In a stand mixer with the paddle attachment, beat the butter and sugar until pale and creamy. Add the melted chocolate and mix until incorporated. While mixing, add the egg yolks, one at a time, mixing well after each addition. Add the vanilla and mix to combine. Sift the flour and baking powder over the mixture and fold them in using a spatula.

4   In a separate bowl, using hand-held electric beaters, whisk the egg whites until stiff peaks form.

5   Gently fold the egg whites into the cake batter. Transfer the mixture to the tin and bake for 13 minutes until the cake is golden on top and a toothpick inserted into the cake comes out clean. Leave the cake to cool in the tin.

6   Purée the 600g (1lb 5oz) whole strawberries in a blender. Transfer the strawberries to a saucepan over medium heat and bring to the boil. Remove the pan from the heat and add the jelly powder, stirring until dissolved. Add the champagne to the saucepan and stir to combine.

7   Set the jelly mixture aside until thickened but not set (you should still be able to pour it). When thick, pour the jelly mixture on top of the cake. Transfer to the fridge.

8   Combine the milk and vanilla seeds in a saucepan and bring to the boil. Remove the pan from the heat and add the remaining 300g (10½oz) chopped white chocolate. Leave for 2 minutes before stirring until the chocolate is melted and the mixture is smooth.

9   In a bowl, mix the gelatine with the cold water and leave for 10 minutes. Add the gelatine to the chocolate mixture and stir until combined. Set the mixture aside to cool.

10 In a separate large bowl using hand-held electric beaters, whip the cream until soft peaks form.

11 Using a spatula, fold the whipped cream into the cooled chocolate mixture.

12 Pour the white chocolate mousse on top of the cake in the tin and refrigerate for 4 hours.

13 Arrange the grated white chocolate and halved strawberries evenly over the top of the cake. Refrigerate for 1 hour. Release from the tin and place on a decorative plate to serve.

14 Store in the fridge for up to 3 days.

This cake is one of my favourites to bake – and eat – because the flavours of almond and coconut in the sponge just complement each other so perfectly.

RAFFAELLO CAKE

ALMOND SPONGE

4 large eggs, room temperature
2 tablespoons warm water
200g (7oz) caster (superfine) sugar
125g (4½oz) plain (all-purpose) flour
1 teaspoon baking powder
pinch of salt
100g (3½oz) almond meal

1. Preheat the oven to 175°C (345°F). Grease the base of a round 20cm (8 inch) springform cake tin and line the base with baking paper.

2. In a stand mixer with the whisk attachment, whisk the eggs, water and sugar until light and fluffy.

3. Sift the flour, baking powder and salt over the mixture and fold them in gently using a spatula.

4. Add the almond meal and fold it in gently, making sure not to overmix as this will cause the cake to be dense.

5. Pour the batter into the tin and level the surface. Bake for 40 minutes until the cake is golden brown on top and a toothpick inserted into the cake comes out clean. Set aside to cool in the tin.

6. Once completely cool, remove from the tin and slice it into three separate layers, horizontally, using a cake wire or a serrated knife.

COCONUT CREAM

250g (9oz) double (thick) cream
200ml (7fl oz) coconut cream
250g (9oz) white chocolate, broken into pieces
1½ tablespoons coconut rum
250g (9oz) mascarpone
100g (3½oz) desiccated coconut

1. Combine the thick cream and coconut cream in a medium saucepan over high heat and bring to the boil.

2. Remove the pan from the heat. Add the white chocolate and coconut rum, leave for 2 minutes, then stir until the chocolate is melted and the mixture is smooth.

3. Cover with plastic wrap touching the surface of the cream, to prevent a skin forming, then refrigerate for 6 hours.

4. Remove from the fridge. In a stand mixer with the whisk attachment, whisk the chilled chocolate with the mascarpone on high speed until the mixture thickens. Add the desiccated coconut and mix to combine.

TOASTED ALMONDS & COCONUT

100g (3½oz) almond flakes
30g (1oz) desiccated (dried shredded)coconut

1 In a dry frying pan over medium heat, toast the almond flakes, tossing often, until golden brown. Set aside to cool completely.

2 Toast the coconut in the same way and set aside to cool completely.

TO ASSEMBLE

150ml (5fl oz) amaretto

1 Place the first sponge cake layer on a cake board or serving plate and soak the sponge with one-third of the amaretto.

2 Spread one-third of the coconut cream over the top of the first cake layer.

3 Top with the second cake layer and soak this with another one-third of the amaretto and spread half of the remaining coconut cream over the top.

4 Top with the final cake layer and soak it with the remaining amaretto.

5 Spread the remaining coconut cream over the top and side of the cake.

6 Sprinkle toasted coconut over the top of the cake (see photograph). Cover the side of the cake with the toasted almond flakes.

7 Chill the cake in the fridge for at least 1 hour before serving.

8 The cake will keep in the fridge for up to 2 days. Serve at room temperature.

JANUSZ SAYS

This cake is named after a chocolate truffle that I'm in love with – Raffaello. It consists of a whole almond surrounded by a creamy coconut filling, all encased in a thin and crispy wafer shell, then coated with white chocolate and shredded coconut. I've added amaretto for an extra kick.

These Earl Grey and lemon, teacup-shaped cookies are as fragrant as they are tasty. They are the perfect treat to snack on while spilling the tea with friends. Just make sure the tea is piping hot!

SPILL-THE-TEA COOKIES

COOKIES

100g (3½oz) unsalted butter, room temperature
50g (1¾oz) caster (superfine) sugar
1 teaspoon vanilla bean paste
leaves from 2 Earl Grey teabags
zest of 1 lemon
150g (5½oz) plain (all-purpose) flour

ICING

1 large pasteurised egg white (pasteurised egg whites in cartons are sold at most supermarkets), room temperature
200g (7oz) icing (confectioners') sugar, sifted
1 teaspoon lemon juice
½ teaspoon blue gel food colouring

1 Grease two baking trays and line them with baking paper.

2 For the cookies, in a stand mixer with the paddle attachment, beat the butter until pale and creamy. While mixing, gradually add the caster sugar, a tablespoon at a time, until fully incorporated. While mixing, add the vanilla, tea and lemon zest and mix until combined.

3 Sift the flour over the mixture and mix until a soft dough forms.

4 Wrap the dough in plastic wrap and refrigerate for 30 minutes.

5 Remove the dough from the fridge and let it rest for 10 minutes.

6 On a floured work surface, roll out the dough until 3mm (⅛ inch) thick. Using a 12–15cm (4½–6 inch) teacup-shaped cookie cutter (or a knife and a template made from card), cut out 18 cookies.

7 Place the cookies on the baking trays and place in the freezer for 15 minutes.

8 Preheat the oven to 180°C (350°F).

9 Remove from the freezer and bake for 10 minutes until the edges are beginning to turn golden brown. Set aside to cool slightly on the trays, then transfer to a wire rack to cool completely.

10 For the icing, in a stand mixer with the whisk attachment, whisk the egg white until stiff peaks form. While whisking, gradually add the icing sugar, a tablespoon at a time, until fully incorporated.

11 Divide the mixture evenly between two bowls. Add ½ teaspoon of the lemon juice to one bowl and mix to combine. Add the remainder of the lemon juice and the blue food colouring to the other bowl and mix until well combined and the colour is even.

12 Transfer the mixture to two separate piping bags with small plain nozzles.

13 Pipe thin white outlines around your teacups.

14 Pipe decorative blue swirls onto your teacups to achieve pretty, vintage patterns (see photograph).

15 Once the icing has dried, store in an airtight container for up to 1 week.

MAKES 30

I couldn't have a chapter on baking for the ones you love and not include a recipe for the love of my life, Nigel, my sausage dog. These rough, hearty banana and peanut butter cookies are a favourite of mine and Nigel's to share. Although I like to think he enjoys them so much because they're made with love, I know it's really because he's obsessed with peanut butter!

DOG-FRIENDLY BANANA & PEANUT BUTTER COOKIES

95g (3¼oz) rolled (porridge) oats
260g (9¼oz) smooth peanut
    butter (xylitol free)
1 banana, mashed
60ml (2fl oz) water

1   Preheat the oven to 180°C (350°F). Grease a baking tray and line it with baking paper.

2   In a large mixing bowl, using your hands, combine the rolled oats, peanut butter, mashed banana and water into a dough.

3   On a floured work surface, roll the dough out until 5mm (¼ inch) thick.

4   Using a cookie cutter of your choice, cut the dough into shapes that your dog will love – for Nigel I shape these treats into little pigs!

5   Place the treats on the baking tray and bake for 15 minutes until golden brown. Set aside to cool slightly on the tray, then transfer to a wire rack to cool completely.

6   Once cool, serve to your dog with a side of belly rubs. Take one for yourself, of course, then store in an airtight container for up to 1 week.

These delightful cookies are a sweet and colourful treat to celebrate Pride Month. Made with a buttery dough, the cookies are flavoured with a hint of cinnamon and orange zest, but the real showstopper is the rainbow icing. Perfect for sharing with friends and loved ones, these cookies are a delicious way to celebrate the LGBTQ+ community.

PRIDE FLAG COOKIES

CINNAMON & ORANGE COOKIES

60g (2¼oz) unsalted butter, cold, cubed
30g (1oz) caster (superfine) sugar
120g (4¼oz) plain (all-purpose) flour, sifted
1 large egg yolk, room temperature
½ teaspoon ground cinnamon
1 teaspoon orange zest

RAINBOW ICING

1 large pasteurised egg white (pasteurised egg whites in cartons are sold at most supermarkets), room temperature
200g (7oz) icing (confectioners') sugar, sifted
1 teaspoon lemon juice
5 drops each of red, orange, yellow, green, blue and purple gel food colouring

1 Grease two baking trays and line them with baking paper.

2 For the cookies, in a stand mixer with the paddle attachment, mix the butter, sugar and flour on low speed until the texture resembles breadcrumbs. Add the egg yolk, cinnamon and orange zest and mix until a stiff dough forms.

3 Wrap the dough in plastic wrap and refrigerate for 1 hour.

4 Remove the dough from the fridge and let it rest for 10 minutes.

5 On a floured work surface, roll out the dough until 3mm (⅛ inch) thick.

6 Cut the dough into 4 x 2cm (1½ x ¾ inch) flags on 8cm (3¼ inch) poles – using either a cookie cutter or a knife and a template made from card.

7 Place the cookies on the trays and freeze for 15 minutes.

8 Preheat the oven to 180°C (350°F).

9 Remove the cookies from the freezer and bake for 10 minutes until the edges are starting to brown. Cool slightly on the trays, then transfer to a wire rack to cool completely.

10 For the icing, in a stand mixer with the whisk attachment, whisk the egg white until stiff peaks form. While whisking, gradually add the sugar, a tablespoon at a time, until fully incorporated. Add the lemon juice and mix to combine.

11 Divide the mixture evenly among six bowls. Add a different food colouring to each one and mix until well combined and the colours are even.

12 Transfer the icing to six separate piping bags with plain nozzles. Pipe the rainbow flag onto the flag part of each cookie.

13 Leave to set for 2–3 hours before serving.

14 Store in an airtight container for up to 1 week.

SERVES 6

Being raised by a feminist mother in Poland and living life as a gay man today, I am constantly inspired by women. Celebrate the power of women with this female power symbol cake, comprised of German vanilla buttercream and passionfruit curd sandwiched between layers of orange blossom-flavoured biscuit and topped with crushed meringue and fresh fruit.

GIRL POWER SYMBOL CAKE

ORANGE BLOSSOM BISCUIT BASE

200g (7oz) plain (all-purpose) flour
125g (4½oz) unsalted butter, cold, cubed
50g (1¾oz) almond meal
50g (1¾oz) icing (confectioners') sugar, sifted
1 teaspoon vanilla bean paste
1 teaspoon orange blossom water
zest of 1 orange

1. Grease two baking trays and line them with baking paper.

2. Place all the ingredients in a stand mixer with the paddle attachment and mix until a stiff dough forms.

3. Wrap the dough in plastic wrap and refrigerate for 30 minutes.

4. Remove the dough from the fridge and let it rest for 10 minutes.

5. On a floured work surface, roll out the dough until 1cm (½ inch) thick.

6. Using a template of the traditional female symbol (I cut mine out of an A4/21 x 30cm/8¼ x 12 inch piece of card), cut out two large biscuits and place one on each tray.

7. Freeze the dough for 15 minutes. Preheat the oven to 180°C (350°F).

8. Remove from the freezer and bake for 12 minutes until the edges are golden brown.

9. Allow the shapes to cool completely to room temperature on the baking trays.

GERMAN VANILLA BUTTERCREAM

2 large egg yolks, room temperature
50g (1¾oz) caster (superfine) sugar
1 tablespoon plain (all-purpose) flour, sifted
1½ tablespoons cornflour (cornstarch), sifted
170ml (5½fl oz) full-cream (whole) milk
1½ teaspoons vanilla bean paste
120g (4¼oz) unsalted butter, room temperature

1. Place the egg yolks, sugar and flours in a bowl and whisk until combined.

2. In a medium saucepan over medium heat, heat the milk and vanilla bean paste until almost boiling.

3. While whisking, add the hot milk to the egg mixture, then transfer the mixture back to the pan and bring to the boil, whisking constantly. Remove the pan from the heat, cover with plastic wrap, touching the surface of the cream, to prevent a skin forming, and set aside to come to room temperature.

4. In a stand mixer with the paddle attachment, beat the butter for 5 minutes until pale and creamy. While mixing, add the room-temperature cream mixture, a tablespoon at a time, mixing well after each addition, until combined.

5. Transfer to a piping bag with a large plain nozzle.

PASSIONFRUIT CURD

2 passionfruit
1 tablespoon lemon juice
2 large egg yolks, room
  temperature
20g (¾oz) unsalted butter
25g (1oz) caster (superfine) sugar

1. Cut the passionfruit in half and scoop out the pulp.

2. Transfer all the ingredients to a small saucepan over medium heat and whisk constantly until boiling.

3. Remove from the heat and pour the mixture into a bowl.

4. Transfer to the fridge to cool.

5. Once the mixture has cooled, transfer it to a piping bag with a small plain nozzle.

TO ASSEMBLE

selection of fresh fruit, sliced
  (I used strawberries, raspberries,
  blackberries, blueberries, kiwi
  fruit and peaches)
10 Rainbow Meringues (page 106)

1. Place the first biscuit on a cake board or serving plate and pipe two rows of individual cream 'blobs' around it (see photograph).

2. Pipe the curd in the gaps between the blobs of cream.

3. Place the second biscuit on top and repeat the piping.

4. Decorate with the fresh sliced fruit, whole meringues and crushed meringues.

5. Eat this on the day you make it.

JANUSZ SAYS

By changing the shape of your cut-out, you can celebrate anything Pride-related, such as non-binary power or transgender power.

SERVES 10

Celebrate your love with this cute mango, kiwi fruit and orange-flavoured vintage heart cake with a personal message piped on top. I love the idea of mixing a modern-day message with a romantic, vintage-style cake. So get modern and down with the kids when thinking about the wording of your message!

MODERN VINTAGE HEART CAKE

MANGO & VANILLA CAKE

170g (6oz) unsalted butter, room temperature
150g (5½oz) caster (superfine) sugar
3 large eggs, room temperature
1 teaspoon vanilla bean paste
350g (12oz) plain (all-purpose) flour
2 teaspoons baking powder
400g (14oz) mango purée

1. Preheat the oven to 170°C (325°F). Grease the base and sides of three 19cm (7½ inch) heart-shaped cake tins and line the bases with baking paper.

2. In a stand mixer with the paddle attachment, beat the butter until pale and creamy. While mixing, gradually add the sugar, a tablespoon at a time, until fully incorporated. While mixing, add the eggs one at a time, mixing well after each addition, then mix in the vanilla.

3. In a separate bowl, mix the flour with the baking powder.

4. Sift half of the flour mixture over the butter mixture and fold it in using a spatula.

5. Add half of the mango purée and fold it in.

6. Repeat steps 4 and 5 with the remaining flour, baking powder and mango purée.

7. Divide the batter evenly among the three tins and level the surface. Bake for 20 minutes until a toothpick inserted into the cakes comes out clean. Cool for 5 minutes in the tins, then transfer to a wire rack to cool completely.

KIWI FRUIT CURD

2 kiwi fruit, peeled
juice of ½ lemon
1 large egg yolk, room temperature
1 large egg, room temperature
40g (1½oz) caster (superfine) sugar
25g (1oz) unsalted butter

1. In a food processor, blend the kiwi fruit and lemon juice until smooth.

2. Transfer to a medium saucepan over medium–high heat, along with the remaining curd ingredients. Bring to the boil, then remove the pan from the heat and set aside to cool.

ORANGE BUTTERCREAM

280g (10oz) unsalted butter, room
temperature
zest of 2 large oranges
280g (10oz) icing (confectioners')
sugar, sifted
1½ teaspoons pink gel food
colouring
560g (1lb 4oz) cream cheese,
room temperature

1   In a stand mixer with the paddle
attachment, beat the butter and
orange zest until pale and creamy.
While mixing, gradually add the
sugar, a tablespoon at a time, until
fully incorporated. Add ½ teaspoon
of the food colouring and mix until
combined and the colour is even.

2   While mixing on low speed, add
the cream cheese in four batches,
mixing well after each addition, until
combined and fluffy. Be careful not
to overmix as it may become watery.

3   Place half of the buttercream
in a bowl, then scoop 4 tablespoons
into a piping bag with a plain nozzle
and set aside. This will be the palest
pink buttercream.

4   Divide the remaining buttercream
between two bowls. Add
¾ teaspoon of pink food colouring
to one bowl and ¼ teaspoon to the
other, so you have two shades of
pink – a baby pink and a hot pink.
Mix each bowl until well combined
and the colours are even.

TO ASSEMBLE

1   Place a heart-shaped sponge
on the centre of a cake board
or serving plate and cover with
one-quarter of the palest pink
buttercream.

2   Pipe a slightly higher border of
buttercream around the outside
of the cake to act as a dam to stop
the curd from leaking out when
you add it.

3   Fill the centre with half the curd.

4   Top with the second sponge and
repeat the process with another
one-quarter of the palest pink
buttercream and the remaining curd.

5   Top with the third sponge, cover the
whole cake with the remaining palest
pink buttercream and smooth using
a cake scraper or palette knife.
Refrigerate for 30 minutes.

6   Place the hot pink buttercream
in a piping bag with a star or
leaf/teardrop nozzle and pipe a
decorative outline around the top
and base of the cake. Pipe a wavy
line around the middle of the cake.

7   Place the baby pink buttercream
into a piping bag with a star or leaf/
teardrop nozzle and pipe outlines
next to the hot pink ones on the top
and base of the cake.

8   Take whichever colour of pink
buttercream that you have left,
transfer it to a piping bag with a small
plain nozzle and pipe a modern
romantic message on top of your
vintage heart cake – I like to write
'XOXO Love ya babes, Hunbun'.

9   Store the cake in the fridge for up to
3 days. Serve at room temperature.

MAKES 16

Brownies and chill, anyone? These chocolate and peanut butter brownies contain sugar-coated peanuts and are topped with salted pretzels. They are perfect for a date night on the sofa with yourself or with the one you love. Using soy sauce in place of salt balances the richness of the brownie and adds an extra layer of umami flavour.

DATE-NIGHT BROWNIES

80g (2¾oz) unsalted butter
125g (4½oz) milk chocolate (35% cocoa solids), chopped
125g (4½oz) dark chocolate (50% cocoa solids), chopped
1 tablespoon vanilla bean paste
150g (5½oz) coconut blossom sugar
1 tablespoon soy sauce
2 large eggs, room temperature
40g (1½oz) cornflour (cornstarch)
30g (1oz) pure unsweetened cocoa powder
100g (3½oz) colourful sugar-coated peanuts
2 tablespoons smooth peanut butter
16 salted pretzels

1   Preheat the oven to 180°C (350°F). Line a 20cm (8 inch) square tin with baking paper.

2   In a medium saucepan over medium heat, melt the butter, both chocolates and the vanilla bean paste. Once melted, remove the pan from the heat, add the sugar, soy sauce and eggs and stir until well combined.

3   Sift the cornflour and cocoa powder over the batter and mix until fully combined.

4   Add the sugar-coated peanuts and ensure they are evenly distributed throughout the mixture.

5   Transfer the batter to the tin and level the surface.

6   Heat the peanut butter in the microwave on High for 10–15 seconds until melted, then pour it over the brownie mixture.

7   Using a toothpick, create a feathered effect in the peanut butter (see photograph), then place the salted pretzels on top, evenly spaced so there will be one per brownie when it is cut into pieces.

8   Bake the brownie for 20 minutes. Remove from the oven and let it rest for 2 hours before slicing and serving.

9   Store in an airtight container at room temperature for up to 3 days. However, if you prefer a fudgy texture, store them in the fridge for up to 1 week.

JANUSZ SAYS

Coconut blossom sugar can be found in many supermarkets. However, it can be easily substituted with a mixture of 50% light brown sugar and 50% dark brown sugar.

For this recipe I wanted to help share the love by throwing it back to the 90s and cooking up a batch of nostalgia. These small, easy-to-make rainbow gems have a sugar cookie base and colourful royal icing tips. They are sure to remind you of simpler times, when the only heartbreak we knew was Geri leaving the Spice Girls.

RAINBOW GEMS

SUGAR COOKIES

75g (2½oz) salted butter, room temperature
35g (1¼oz) golden caster (superfine) sugar
¼ teaspoon almond essence
110g (3¾oz) plain (all-purpose) flour, plus extra for rolling

1 Grease two baking trays and line them with baking paper.

2 In a stand mixer with the paddle attachment, beat the butter on high speed, gradually adding the sugar, a tablespoon at a time, until the mixture is pale and creamy and the sugar is fully incorporated. Add the almond essence, sift the flour over the mixture and mix on low speed until a stiff dough forms.

3 Wrap the dough in plastic wrap and refrigerate for 30 minutes.

4 Remove the dough from the fridge and let it rest for 10 minutes.

5 On a lightly floured work surface, roll the dough out until 5mm (¼ inch) thick. Using a 2cm (¾ inch) round cookie cutter, cut out 80 circles.

6 Transfer the circles to the baking trays and refrigerate for 30 minutes. Preheat the oven to 180°C (350°F).

7 Remove from the fridge and bake for 9 minutes until slightly golden. Leave to cool for a few minutes on the trays, then transfer to a wire rack to cool completely.

RAINBOW ICING

5g (⅛oz) egg white powder
4 tablespoons warm water
½ teaspoon natural vanilla extract
250g (9oz) icing (confectioners') sugar, sifted
⅛ teaspoon each of red, orange, yellow, green, blue and purple gel food colouring

1 In a stand mixer with the whisk attachment, combine the egg white powder with 2 tablespoons of the warm water, mixing to form a thick paste. While whisking, gradually add the remaining warm water and the vanilla, mixing until stiff peaks form. While whisking, gradually add the icing sugar, a tablespoon at a time, until fully incorporated.

2 Divide the icing evenly among six bowls. Add a different food colouring to each bowl and mix until well combined and the colours are even.

3 Transfer each coloured icing to a separate piping bag with a star nozzle.

TO ASSEMBLE

1 Separate the baked cookies into six batches, piping a rosette of a different-coloured icing onto the cookies in each batch.

2 Set the cookies aside to dry for 2 hours before serving.

3 The cookies will keep in an airtight container for up to 1 week.

This apple rosette tart consists of an almond pastry crust filled with a rich vanilla custard cream, then topped with apple slices rolled to resemble roses. It is full of flavour and is perfect to bake for somebody you love who prefers cake to flowers!

APPLE ROSETTE TART

ALMOND PASTRY

60g (2¼oz) unsalted butter, chilled, cubed
100g (3½oz) plain (all-purpose) flour, sifted
30g (1oz) almond meal
40g (1½oz) icing (confectioners') sugar
1 large egg yolk, room temperature
½ teaspoon almond essence
1 teaspoon water

1 Preheat the oven to 180°C (350°F).

2 In a food processor, mix the butter, flour, almond meal and sugar until the texture resembles breadcrumbs. Add the egg yolk, almond essence and water and mix until a stiff dough forms.

3 Wrap the dough in plastic wrap and refrigerate for 30 minutes.

4 Remove the dough from the fridge and set aside for 10 minutes.

5 On a floured work surface, roll out the pastry until it's large enough to line a 19cm (7½ inch) flan (tart) tin.

6 Transfer the pastry to the tin and freeze for 20 minutes.

7 Remove from the freezer. Cover the pastry with baking paper, fill with baking beans and bake for 15 minutes.

8 Remove the paper and the beans and return the tart to the oven for a further 10 minutes until lightly golden. Leave to cool in the tin.

CUSTARD CREAM FILLING

4 large egg yolks, room temperature
80g (2¾oz) caster (superfine) sugar
25g (1oz) plain (all-purpose) flour
25g (1oz) cornflour (cornstarch)
400ml (14fl oz) full-cream (whole) milk
2 teaspoons vanilla bean paste

1 In a bowl, using hand-held electric beaters, whisk the egg yolks and sugar on high speed until light and fluffy. Sift the flour and cornflour over the mixture and whisk to combine.

2 Combine the milk and vanilla in a medium saucepan over medium heat and bring almost to the boil.

3 While whisking, add the hot milk to the egg mixture, then return all the mixture to the pan. While whisking, heat the mixture until it boils and thickens.

4 Transfer the mixture into the pastry case and level the surface.

APPLE ROSETTES

5 pink lady apples, unpeeled
500ml (17fl oz) water
200g (7oz) caster (superfine)
  sugar
juice of 2 lemons

1 Core the apples and cut them into quarters.

2 Slice the quarters into 2mm (1/16 inch) slices using a mandoline or sharp knife.

3 In a large saucepan over high heat, bring the water, sugar and lemon juice to the boil. Add the apple slices and cook for 1 minute. Remove the apples from the pan to prevent overcooking.

4 Arrange six slices of apples on a plate so that they overlap each other by half.

5 Starting at the first slice, roll it up to form a rose shape. Repeat with the remaining apple.

TO ASSEMBLE

1 As you finish each apple rose, place it on the tart, pressing it firmly into the custard.

2 Repeat the process until there are no gaps – any small gaps can be filled by rolling two or three slices of apple together and pressing them into the gaps.

3 Remove the tart from the tin before serving.

4 Store in the fridge for up to 24 hours. Best served at room temperature.

JANUSZ SAYS

This tart is a variation on a French apple tart that is made with several overlapping layers of apple slices. This version, made with the rosettes, is just as delicious and much quicker to make.

MAKES ABOUT 120

Although simple, these cute, colourful meringues are fun and delicious. They can be eaten with fruit and fresh cream or ice cream, or used to decorate a number of the bakes in this book ... that is, if you don't eat them all first!

RAINBOW MERINGUES

3 large egg whites, room temperature
¼ teaspoon cream of tartar
180g (6½oz) caster (superfine) sugar
2 drops each of red, orange, yellow, green, blue and purple gel food colouring

1 Preheat the oven to 140°C (275°F). Grease two baking trays and line them with baking paper.

2 In a stand mixer with the whisk attachment, whisk the egg whites until frothy. Add the cream of tartar and whisk until stiff peaks form. While whisking, gradually add the sugar, a tablespoon at a time, and mix until the sugar is fully incorporated and the mixture is no longer grainy.

3 Place two uncut disposable piping bags inside two large tall glasses and fold the top of the bag over the rim of the glass. Place a star nozzle into the tip of each one. You now have two glasses lined with piping bags. Dip a toothpick in one of the gel colours and draw a couple of random lines up the inside of the piping bag. Repeat with fresh toothpicks and the other colours. (When you pipe the meringue mixture, it will now come out in striped rainbow colours.) Repeat with the second piping bag.

4 Transfer the meringue mixture into the piping bags and cut the tip to expose the nozzle. Pipe your star-shaped meringues (about 1cm/½ inch in size) onto the trays.

5 Bake for 45 minutes. Set aside to cool before serving.

6 Store in an airtight container for up to 2 weeks.

JANUSZ SAYS

These meringues make beautiful decorations for your baked goods. You can use them to decorate your cakes and desserts, or just leave them on the table to add more colour to it. I use these to decorate my Girl Power Symbol Cake on page 94.

Celebrate the special people in your life on their special day with this camp and cute recipe. This birthday cake with a twist comprises layers of Victoria sponge and raspberry jam-flavoured fudge topped with vanilla frosting and rainbow sprinkles. Decoratively wrapped, this fudge makes a perfect gift.

BIRTHDAY CAKE FUDGE

500ml (17fl oz) condensed milk
4 tablespoons store-bought vanilla cake mix
550g (1lb 4oz) white chocolate, chopped
2 teaspoons raspberry jelly (gelatine dessert) powder
1 teaspoon vanilla bean paste
⅛ teaspoon white gel food colouring
2 tablespoons rainbow sprinkles

1   Line a deep 15cm (6 inch) square cake tin with baking paper.

2   Combine 150ml (5fl oz) of the condensed milk and 2 tablespoons of the cake mix in a saucepan over medium–high heat and bring to the boil, stirring.

3   Remove the pan from the heat. Add 170g (6oz) of the white chocolate and leave to sit for 2 minutes, then stir until the chocolate is melted and the mixture is smooth.

4   Transfer the mixture to the tin and level the surface.

5   Place in the freezer for 10 minutes.

6   Place 100ml (3½fl oz) of the condensed milk in a saucepan and bring to the boil.

7   Remove the pan from the heat, add the jelly powder and mix until dissolved. Add 100g (3½oz) of the white chocolate, leave to sit for 2 minutes, then stir until the chocolate is melted and the mixture is smooth.

8   Remove the tin from the freezer. Pour the jelly mixture on top of the first layer of fudge in the tin and level the surface. Transfer to the freezer for a further 10 minutes.

9   Combine 150ml (5fl oz) of the condensed milk and the remaining cake mix in a saucepan and bring to the boil, stirring.

10   Remove the pan from the heat. Add 170g (6oz) of the white chocolate and leave to sit for 2 minutes, then stir until the chocolate is melted and the mixture is smooth.

11   Remove the tin from the freezer. Pour the chocolate mixture on top of the raspberry layer of fudge in the tin and level the surface. Transfer to the freezer for a further 10 minutes.

12   Combine the remaining condensed milk, vanilla bean paste and white food colouring in a saucepan over medium–high heat and bring to the boil, stirring.

13   Remove the pan from the heat. Add the remaining white chocolate and leave to sit for 2 minutes, then stir until the chocolate is melted and the mixture is smooth.

14   Remove the tin from the freezer and pour the last chocolate layer on top.

15   Scatter with the sprinkles and leave to set for 4 hours at room temperature.

16   Remove from the tin and cut into squares before serving.

17   Store in an airtight container at room temperature for up to 2 weeks. Do not refrigerate as it will lose its texture.

MAKES 12

These tarts celebrate the classic lemon meringue pie, but with a twist – a meringue 'lemon' on top. They are sweet enough to gift to the people you love, but are also bitter enough to gift to those you've left behind as a reminder of what they're missing!

MINI LEMON MERINGUE TARTS

PASTRY

60g (2¼oz) unsalted butter, room temperature
50g (1¾oz) icing (confectioners') sugar
110g (3¾oz) plain (all-purpose) flour
1 large egg yolk, room temperature
1 teaspoon vanilla bean paste
pinch of salt

1   In a stand mixer with the paddle attachment, mix all the ingredients on low speed until a smooth dough forms.

2   Wrap the dough in plastic wrap and refrigerate for 30 minutes.

3   Remove the dough from the fridge and divide it into 12 equal portions.

4   Roll each portion into a ball, then place them into 12 individual 5cm (2½ inch) mini flan (tart) tins, pressing the dough into the sides of the tins.

5   Place the tins in the freezer for 10 minutes. Preheat the oven to 190°C (375°F).

6   Remove the tins from the freezer and place a piece of baking paper on top of each dough case and fill with baking beans.

7   Bake for 6 minutes. Remove the paper and beans, then return to the oven to bake for a further 5 minutes until golden. Set aside to cool in the tins completely.

LEMON CURD

zest and juice of 2 lemons
juice of 1 small orange
2 large egg yolks, room temperature
40g (1½oz) unsalted butter
80g (2¾oz) caster (superfine) sugar
1 tablespoon cornflour (cornstarch)

1   Combine all the ingredients in a medium saucepan over medium heat. Stirring constantly, bring to the boil, cook for around 30 seconds, then remove from the heat.

2   Cover with plastic wrap touching the surface of the curd, to prevent a skin forming, then set aside to cool.

3   When cool, spoon the curd equally among the pastry cases.

MERINGUE

3 egg whites, room temperature
¼ teaspoon cream of tartar
150g (5½oz) caster (superfine)
  sugar
2 teaspoons yellow gel food
  colouring
1 drop of orange gel food colouring

1 Preheat the oven to 150°C (300°F). Place the 12 tart tins on a large baking tray.

2 In a stand mixer with the whisk attachment, whisk the egg whites until foamy. Add the cream of tartar and whisk until stiff peaks form. While whisking, gradually add the sugar, a tablespoon at a time, until fully incorporated. Add the food colourings and whisk until fully combined and the colour is even.

3 Transfer the meringue mixture to a piping bag with a large plain nozzle.

4 Pipe the meringue onto the lemon curd in a 7–8cm (2¾–3¼ inch) dome with a peak, to resemble half a lemon.

5 Bake the tarts for 10 minutes, then set aside to cool in the tin.

TO ASSEMBLE

12 small mint leaves

1 Once cool, top each tart with a small mint leaf and serve.

2 Store in an airtight container in the fridge for up to 2 days. Serve at room temperature.

JANUSZ SAYS

You can easily transform lemon curd into kiwi fruit curd by using the recipe from my Modern Vintage Heart Cake on page 98. Or try a lemon–lime flavour by substituting 1 lemon with the juice and zest of 2 limes.

HOMe
PRIDe

This fun, colourful cake is inspired by the pride I have for the city I live in – Brighton! The vibrant jade colour can be seen throughout the city and the mint-chocolate flavour and ice cream drip decoration celebrate one of my favourite things to do here – eat mint choc chip ice cream on the beach in summer.

JANUSZ'S BRIGHTON CAKE

CHOCOLATE SPONGE

100g (3½oz) unsalted butter
65g (2¼oz) dark chocolate
  (70% cocoa solids), chopped
60g (2¼oz) pure unsweetened
  cocoa powder
2 large eggs, room temperature
1 large egg yolk, room temperature
1 tablespoon natural vanilla extract
300g (10½oz) dark brown sugar
50ml (1½fl oz) vegetable oil
160g (5½oz) plain (all-purpose) flour
1 teaspoon baking powder
½ teaspoon bicarbonate of soda
  (baking soda)
¼ teaspoon salt
160ml (5¼fl oz) buttermilk

1   Preheat the oven to 170°C (325°F). Generously grease four 15cm (6 inch) round cake tins and line them with baking paper.

2   Melt the butter and chocolate in a small saucepan over medium–low heat, stirring constantly. Once the chocolate has melted, remove the pan from the heat. Add the cocoa powder and stir until combined.

3   In a stand mixer with the whisk attachment, whisk the eggs, egg yolk, vanilla, sugar and oil on high speed for 5 minutes.

4   Add the slightly cooled butter mixture and fold in by hand to combine.

5   Sift the flour, baking powder, bicarbonate of soda and salt into a bowl and mix briefly to combine.

6   Using a spatula, gradually fold in half of the flour mixture, then half of the buttermilk. Repeat with the remaining flour mixture and buttermilk.

7   Divide the batter evenly among the tins and level the surface. Bake for 25 minutes, or until a toothpick inserted into the cakes comes out clean. Leave to cool in the tins.

MINT CHOCOLATE FILLING

200g (7oz) double (thick) cream
200g (7oz) mascarpone
⅛ teaspoon jade gel food colouring
50g (1¾oz) icing (confectioners')
  sugar, sifted
¾ teaspoon mint essence
50g (1¾oz) chocolate chips
  (50% cocoa solids)

1   In a stand mixer with the whisk attachment, whip the cream, mascarpone, food colouring and sugar until thickened. Add the mint essence and chocolate chips and fold them in using a spatula. Set aside.

JADE MINT BUTTERCREAM

200g (7oz) unsalted butter, room
  temperature
½ teaspoon mint essence
200g (7oz) condensed milk
1 teaspoon jade gel food colouring

1   In a stand mixer with the paddle attachment, beat the butter and mint essence until pale and creamy. While mixing, add the condensed milk and food colouring.

2   Mix on the lowest speed for 2 minutes to remove any excess air. Alternatively, you can fold the buttercream using a spatula pressing it against the sides of the bowl to remove air bubbles.

WHITE CHOCOLATE DRIP

2 tablespoons double (thick) cream
100g (3½oz) white chocolate, chopped

1 Heat the cream in a small saucepan over medium heat until almost boiling.

2 Remove the pan from the heat. Add the white chocolate and leave to sit for 2 minutes, then stir until the chocolate is melted and the mixture is smooth.

TO ASSEMBLE

100ml (3½fl oz) crème de menthe liqueur
20 edible chocolate pebbles
1 wafer ice cream cone
rainbow sprinkles (optional)

1 Use a cake wire or serrated knife to level the top of each sponge and set the trimmings aside (you'll need them later).

2 Drizzle one-quarter of the crème de menthe evenly over each sponge.

3 Place the first sponge in the centre of a 25cm (10 inch) cake board or serving plate. Add one-third of the mint chocolate filling and spread it over the top of the cake evenly.

4 Top with the second sponge and add another one-third of the mint chocolate filling. Repeat with the third sponge and the last of the mint chocolate filling.

5 Top with the fourth sponge.

6 Refrigerate the cake for 30 minutes.

7 Remove the cake from the fridge and spread an even layer of the jade buttercream over the top and side of the cake, smoothing it using a cake scraper or palette knife.

8 Refrigerate the cake for 1 hour.

9 Mix the cake trimmings with the left-over buttercream to make a cake pop – this will form the 'ice cream' for your cone. Roll the mixture up into a nice, tight ball that will fit snugly on top of the wafer cone. Set aside.

10 Place the 'ice cream' ball in the centre of the cake, or just off-centre. Using a spoon or a piping bottle, run the lukewarm white chocolate drip around the edge of the cake (see photograph) – it needs to be lukewarm and not hot so you do not melt the buttercream. Now cover the ice cream cake pop with the white chocolate drip and cover the top of the cake up to the drip edges.

11 Spread the chocolate pebbles evenly on top of the cake, nestling them into the white chocolate drip.

12 Place the wafer ice cream cone on top of the white chocolate-covered ball – you may have to hold it in place for a few seconds to make sure it sticks to the chocolate. Decorate the top of the ball/cake with sprinkles, if desired.

13 Store in the fridge for up to 2 days but serve at room temperature.

JANUSZ SAYS

Chocolate pebbles are candy-coated chocolate pebbles of different colours and sizes that look like the real thing. If you can't find them, just use whatever chocolate or candy pebbles you can find.

MAKES 12

These marshmallow-stuffed ice cream cones, drizzled in strawberry sauce and topped with rainbow sprinkles, are simple and easy to make. They were a favourite childhood snack of mine in Poland, when we holidayed by the beach, and are something I still think about every summer while walking past Brighton beach's ice cream stands.

marshmallow cones

100g (3½oz) egg whites, room temperature
350g (12oz) caster (superfine) sugar
1 tablespoon vanilla bean paste
60ml (2fl oz) water
12 wafer ice cream cones
rainbow sprinkles
60ml (2fl oz) store-bought strawberry sauce
12 Flake 99s (mini Flakes)

1 Place the egg whites, sugar, vanilla bean paste and water in a glass or metal bowl and whisk until frothy.

2 Place the bowl on top of a pan of simmering water, ensuring the water is not touching the base of the bowl. Using hand-held electric beaters, whisk on high speed for 12 minutes until the temperature of the mixture reaches 70°C (158°F) on a sugar thermometer. Set aside to cool.

3 Transfer the mixture to a piping bag with a large star nozzle.

4 Pipe the mixture into the base of the ice cream cones, spiralling the mixture up into a peak once you reach the top, to achieve a decorative ice cream effect.

5 Place the cones in the fridge, standing upright, to chill.

6 Take the ice cream cones out of the fridge and scatter some rainbow sprinkles on top, add some strawberry sauce and insert a chocolate Flake. Stand the cones upright to set.

7 Once set, serve the cones immediately or store in the fridge, upright, until ready to serve.

8 Store in the fridge for up to 3 days. Serve at room temperature.

JANUSZ SAYS

If you prefer, you can coat your marshmallow cones in chocolate. Melt 250g (9oz) of chocolate with 2 tablespoons of vegetable oil, then dip your cooled cones into the mixture. For serving and storing these cones upright, you can purchase an ice-cream holder online, or simply place each one in a tall glass.

In this fun Polish classic, cherries and whipped cream are sandwiched between two kirsch-soaked sponges and topped with colourful chocolate ganache, whipped cream and a cherry.

BOOZY CHOCOLATE & CHERRY WUZETKA

CHOCOLATE SPONGE

4 large eggs, room temperature, separated
⅛ teaspoon salt
100g (3½oz) caster (superfine) sugar
50g (1¾oz) soft light brown sugar
2 teaspoons natural vanilla extract
60ml (2fl oz) sunflower oil
100g (3½oz) plain (all-purpose) flour
30g (1oz) pure unsweetened cocoa powder
½ teaspoon baking powder

1   Preheat the oven to 170°C (325°F). Grease the bases of the holes in a six-hole mini cake tin (7 x 3cm/ 2¾ x 1¼ inches deep) and line the bases with baking paper.

2   In a stand mixer with the whisk attachment, whisk the egg whites and salt until stiff peaks form.

3   While whisking, gradually add the sugars, a tablespoon at a time, over a period of 5 minutes, until fully incorporated.

4   In a separate bowl, whisk the egg yolks, vanilla and oil until well combined.

5   Whisking on medium speed, add the egg yolk mixture in a steady stream to the egg white mixture and mix until combined.

6   Combine the flour, cocoa and baking powder in a bowl.

7   Sift one-quarter of the dry mixture over the wet mixture and fold it in gently using a spatula. Repeat, one-quarter at a time, with the remaining dry mixture.

8   Divide the mixture evenly among the six holes in the tin and bake for 11 minutes until a toothpick inserted into the cakes comes out clean.

9   Once baked, drop the cake tin onto the bench from a small height to settle the cakes evenly.

10 Set aside to cool for 10 minutes, then remove the cakes from the tin.

11 Use a cake wire or serrated knife to level the tops of the cakes, ensuring they are the same height.

JANUSZ SAYS

Wuzetka is a classic Polish cake that originated in Warsaw during World War II. It consists of chocolate sponges soaked with vodka, filled with whipped cream and topped with a glossy chocolate glaze.

STABILISED WHIPPED CREAM FILLING

1 platinum gelatine leaf
50ml (1½fl oz) water
600g (1lb 5oz) double (thick) cream
50g (1¾oz) icing (confectioners') sugar
1 teaspoon vanilla bean paste

1 Soak the gelatine in the water for 10 minutes.

2 Squeeze the excess water from the gelatine, then melt the gelatine by heating it in the microwave on High for 5 seconds.

3 In a stand mixer with the whisk attachment, whip the cream, icing sugar and vanilla bean paste until soft peaks form. Add the gelatine and whisk again to incorporate.

4 Place 100g (3½ oz) of the cream to a piping bag with a large star nozzle, then transfer the remaining cream to a piping bag with a large plain nozzle. Keep refrigerated until ready to assemble the cake.

WHITE CHOCOLATE GANACHE

35g (1¼oz) double (thick) cream
100g (3½oz) white chocolate, chopped
red, orange, yellow, green, blue and purple gel food colouring

1 Heat the cream in a small saucepan over medium heat. When almost boiling, remove the pan from the heat. Add the white chocolate, wait for 2 minutes, then stir until combined.

2 Divide the mixture evenly among six bowls and add one drop of a different colour to each bowl. Mix well until combined and the colours are even.

TO ASSEMBLE

150g (5½oz) black cherries in kirsch, plus 240ml (8fl oz) kirsch
6 glacé cherries with stems attached

1 Cut each sponge in half horizontally and drizzle kirsch over all the halves.

2 Pipe a border of whipped cream around the top edge of the first sponge using the piping bag with the plain nozzle. Spoon one-sixth of the black cherries into the centre of the whipped cream circle.

3 Place a second sponge on top of the cream and cherries and apply pressure to spread the cream and to secure the sponge in place. Repeat this process until you have six mini cakes.

4 Using a teaspoon, spread a different-coloured white chocolate ganache on top of each cake.

5 Refrigerate the cakes for 30 minutes.

6 Pipe a rosette on top of each cake using the piping bag with the star nozzle, then garnish each one with a glacé cherry.

7 Store in the fridge for up to 2 days. Serve at room temperature.

This rich honey cake is the pride of Poland and was once named one of the best cakes in the world. It has thin layers of baked honey cake soaked in rum and honey, which are filled with indulgent caramel cream, then topped with ganache and walnuts.

POLISH HONEY CAKE

HONEY CAKE

120g (4¼oz) salted butter, room temperature
80g (2¾oz) soft brown sugar
150g (5½oz) runny honey
1 large egg, room temperature
1 teaspoon vanilla bean paste
450g (1lb) plain (all-purpose) flour
1½ teaspoons bicarbonate of soda (baking soda)

1   Preheat the oven to 170°C (325°F). Line the base of a 23cm (9 inch) round springform cake tin with baking paper and grease the sides.

2   In a stand mixer with the paddle attachment, beat the butter until pale and creamy. While mixing, gradually add the sugar and honey and mix until combined. Add the egg and vanilla bean paste and mix to combine.

3   Combine the flour and bicarbonate of soda in a bowl.

4   Sift the flour mixture over the wet mixture, then mix on the lowest speed until a dough forms.

5   Divide the dough into seven equal portions and roll into balls.

6   On a floured work surface, roll out each dough ball to fit in the tin. You can do this by drawing a 23cm (9 inch) circle on a piece of baking paper and using that as a guide, or you can press the dough balls, one by one, into the base of the tin to make them the right size. Bake each portion in the tin individually for 12 minutes. Transfer the baked layers to a wire rack.

RUM & HONEY SOAK

50ml (1½fl oz) runny honey
50ml (1½fl oz) dark spiced rum

1   In a small bowl or cup, mix the honey with the rum until dissolved.

CARAMEL CREAM

500ml (17fl oz) full-cream (whole) milk
40g (1½oz) caster (superfine) sugar
6 large egg yolks, room temperature
25g (1oz) plain (all-purpose) flour, sifted
20g (¾oz) cornflour (cornstarch), sifted
250g (9oz) unsalted butter, room temperature
400g (14oz) dulce de leche (tinned caramel)
100g (3½oz) walnuts, finely chopped

1   Heat the milk in a saucepan over medium heat until almost boiling.

2   Combine the sugar, egg yolks, flour and cornflour in a bowl. While whisking, gradually add half the hot milk to the egg mixture and mix to combine.

3   Transfer all the mixture back to the pan and bring to the boil, whisking constantly.

4   Remove the pan from the heat and cover the mixture with plastic wrap, touching the surface of the caramel cream, to prevent a skin forming. Set aside to cool to room temperature.

5   In a stand mixer with the paddle attachment, beat the butter until pale and creamy. While mixing on medium–low speed, gradually add the cooled egg and milk mixture and continue mixing until just combined – do not overmix or the mixture may curdle. While mixing, gradually add the dulce de leche and mix until combined. Add the chopped nuts and fold them in using a spatula.

CHOCOLATE GANACHE

50g (1¾oz) double (thick) cream
90g (3¼oz) dark chocolate (70% cocoa solids), chopped

1   Heat the cream in a small saucepan over medium heat until almost boiling.

2   Remove the pan from the heat. Add the chocolate and leave to sit for 2 minutes, then stir until the chocolate is melted and the mixture is smooth. Leave the chocolate to cool, but don't let it set.

TO ASSEMBLE

12 walnut halves

1   Place the first sponge layer on a cake board or serving plate and use a pastry brush to soak it with one-sixth of the rum and honey soak.

2   Spread one-sixth of the caramel cream over the top of the soaked sponge.

3   Place the next sponge on top, brush with another one-sixth of the rum and honey soak, add another one-sixth of the caramel cream and spread it over the cake.

4   Repeat until you have placed the sixth layer on top of the cake. Don't add the soak and caramel cream to this layer just yet. Set the seventh cake aside for later.

5   Place a board on top of the cake and place something heavy (like a tin of beans) on top to apply pressure.

6   Transfer to the fridge for 2 hours.

7   Remove the cake from the fridge and remove the weight. Use a pastry brush to apply the remaining rum and honey soak. Spread the remaining cream evenly over the top and side of the cake.

8   Blitz the left-over sponge layer in a food processor to a crumb texture.

9   Press the cake crumbs onto the side of the cake (see photograph).

10   Spread the chocolate ganache evenly over the top of the cake and decorate with the walnuts.

11   Store in the fridge for up to 5 days. Serve at room temperature.

Surprisingly to some, doughnuts are huge in Poland. You cannot visit a market or town in Poland without seeing a display of beautifully decorated doughnuts. This recipe is for a classic fried Polish doughnut, filled with the most popular Polish filling – rose preserve – topped with pink icing and edible dried rose petals.

POLISH ROSE DOUGHNUTS

350g (12oz) plain (all-purpose) flour, sifted
175ml (5½fl oz) full-cream (whole) milk
7g (¼oz) active dried yeast
50g (1¾oz) caster (superfine) sugar
3 large egg yolks, room temperature
1 teaspoon vanilla bean paste
pinch of salt
1 tablespoon orange zest
1 tablespoon white vinegar
35g (1¼oz) unsalted butter, melted and cooled
12 teaspoons rose preserve (stiff)
1 litre (35fl oz) vegetable oil, for frying
70g (2½oz) icing (confectioners') sugar
1½ tablespoons hot water
two drops pink gel food colouring
edible dried rose petals

1 In a stand mixer with the dough hook attachment, mix the flour, milk, yeast, caster sugar, egg yolks, vanilla bean paste, salt, orange zest and vinegar for 8 minutes on medium speed. Add the melted butter and mix for a further 5 minutes until a sticky dough forms.

2 Cover the bowl and leave to prove in a warm place for 90 minutes.

3 Punch the dough down and knead it briefly on a floured work surface.

4 Divide the dough into 12 equal portions and roll them into balls.

5 On a floured work surface, roll out each ball into a 1cm (½ inch) thick circle.

6 Place 1 teaspoon of rose preserve in the centre of each circle. Fold the edges of the dough over the preserve to seal, then reroll into balls.

7 Set the balls aside on a floured work surface in a warm place to prove for 25 minutes.

8 Heat the vegetable oil in a deep frying pan or deep-fryer to 175°C (345°F).

9 Fry the doughnuts in batches in the hot oil, turning them over once, until they are golden brown on both sides. Transfer to a plate lined with paper towel to cool.

10 In a medium bowl, mix the icing sugar with the hot water and the food colouring until smooth and an even colour.

11 Holding a cooled doughnut at both edges, dip one side of the doughnut into the bowl of coloured icing. Transfer to a wire rack set over a sheet of baking paper to catch any drips, then sprinkle with edible rose petals. Leave to set before serving.

12 The doughnuts are best eaten on the day of baking, but they can be stored in an airtight container at room temperature for 24 hours.

MAKES 6

This recipe was inspired by a holiday to Dublin – home of the classic Irish stout – with my partner in 2019. The muffins are chocolate and stout-flavoured, topped with whipped cream and garnished with a white chocolate four-leaf clover to bring you the luck of the Irish.

IRISH GUINNESS MUFFINS

MUFFINS

275g (9¾oz) plain (all-purpose) flour
2 teaspoons bicarbonate of soda (baking soda)
1 teaspoon baking powder
½ teaspoon salt
80g (2¾oz) pure unsweetened cocoa powder
2 large eggs, room temperature
350g (12oz) soft dark brown sugar
250ml (9fl oz) buttermilk
125ml (4fl oz) vegetable oil
1 teaspoon vanilla bean paste
250ml (9fl oz) Guinness

1   Preheat the oven to 180°C (350°F). Generously grease a six-hole jumbo muffin tin (each hole needs a 250ml/ 9fl oz capacity).

2   Combine the flour, bicarbonate of soda, baking powder, salt and cocoa powder in a mixing bowl.

3   In a separate large bowl, whisk together the eggs, sugar, buttermilk, oil and vanilla using hand-held electric beaters.

4   Sift the dry ingredients over the wet ingredients and whisk until combined. Add the Guinness and whisk until combined.

5   Distribute the batter evenly between the six holes of the tin and bake for 30 minutes until a skewer inserted into the muffins comes out clean. Cool in the tin for 5 minutes, then transfer to a wire rack to cool completely.

WHIPPED CREAM TOPPING

250g (9oz) double (thick) cream
100g (3½oz) mascarpone
50g (1¾oz) icing (confectioners') sugar, sifted
¼ teaspoon ground cinnamon
1 teaspoon vanilla bean paste

1   In a stand mixer with the whisk attachment, whip the cream, mascarpone, sugar, cinnamon and vanilla bean paste until soft peaks form.

2   Transfer the cream to a piping bag with a plain nozzle.

FOUR-LEAF CLOVERS

30g (1oz) green-coloured vanilla candy buttons for melting

1   Draw the outline of six four-leaf clovers on baking paper, about 7cm (2¾ inches) in diameter.

2   Heat the candy in the microwave on High in 15-second bursts, stirring after each burst, until melted.

3   Transfer the melted chocolate to a piping bag with a small plain nozzle and pipe over the clover shapes. Leave to one side until set, then peel them off the baking paper.

TO ASSEMBLE

1   Pipe the whipped cream onto the muffins and top with a four-leafed clover.

2   Store in an airtight container in the fridge for up to 2 days.

MAKES 6

A Polish delicacy, these tasty, fluffy, steamed buns are simple to make but have a big impact. The texture is similar to that of a doughnut but these buns are steamed, not fried, and there's even a fruit sauce, so they must be healthy ... right?

POLISH STEAMED BUNS

STEAMED BUNS
250g (9oz) strong flour, sifted
7g (¼oz) active dried yeast
pinch of salt
25g (1oz) caster (superfine) sugar
125ml (4fl oz) full-cream (whole)
   milk, lukewarm
½ teaspoon vanilla bean paste
4 large egg yolks, room
   temperature
25g (1oz) unsalted butter, melted
   and cooled

BLUEBERRY COULIS
250g (9oz) fresh blueberries
30g (1oz) caster (superfine)
   sugar
1 tablespoon lemon juice

HONEY CRÈME FRAÎCHE
250ml (9fl oz) crème fraîche
2 tablespoons runny honey
1 teaspoon vanilla bean paste

1   For the buns, in a stand mixer with the dough hook attachment, mix the flour and yeast to combine. Add the salt, sugar, milk, vanilla bean paste and egg yolks and mix on medium speed until a sticky dough forms.

2   Add the melted butter and mix until a smooth and soft dough forms.

3   Shape the dough into a ball and place it in a floured bowl. Cover and leave to prove in a warm place for 90 minutes until doubled in size.

4   Punch the dough down and knead it briefly on a floured work surface.

5   Divide the dough into six equal portions. Form each portion into a ball and leave to rest on the floured surface for 25 minutes until doubled in size again.

6   Fill a wide saucepan over high heat one-quarter full with water and place a bamboo steamer on top of the pan. Bring the water to the boil. Reduce the heat to low so the water is simmering, then place the risen dough balls into the steamer, leaving plenty of space between them as they will expand during cooking. (You may have to steam them in batches.)

7   Cover and steam the dough balls for 10 minutes. Remove and set aside to cool on a plate.

8   For the blueberry coulis, combine the blueberries, sugar and lemon juice in a medium saucepan over medium heat and simmer for 15 minutes until the fruit is falling apart and the mixture thickens. Blend with a hand-held blender until smooth.

9   Pass the mixture through a fine-mesh strainer into a bowl, discarding the skins and seeds.

10   For the honey crème fraîche, in a medium bowl, mix the crème fraîche with the honey and vanilla bean paste until well combined.

11   To serve, place a warm bun on a small plate, top with the crème fraîche mixture and blueberry coulis and enjoy immediately while hot.

SERVES 12

This orange-flavoured sponge cake is soaked with orange syrup and contains slices of satsuma. The frosting – including the beautiful rainbow world map – is vanilla flavour, voted the world's most loved flavour – a reminder that we can ALL show love and appreciation for the same thing, no matter where we are in the world.

WORLD PRIDE CAKE

SATSUMA SOAK

120g (4¼oz) caster (superfine) sugar
80ml (2½fl oz) water
4 satsumas or mandarins, skin on and cut into 5mm (¼ inch) slices

1 Combine the sugar and water in a saucepan over medium heat and, without stirring, bring it to the boil.

2 Add the satsuma slices and cook for 15 minutes on low heat.

3 Remove the satsumas from the pan. Reserve the cooking liquid as it will be used to soak the cakes once baked. The slices will be used to line the tin.

ORANGE SPONGE

cooked satsuma slices (see above)
3 large eggs, room temperature
180g (6½oz) soft light brown sugar
110g (3¾oz) unsalted butter, melted and cooled
1 teaspoon vanilla bean paste
1 tablespoon orange zest
220g (7¾oz) plain (all-purpose) flour
1 teaspoon bicarbonate of soda (baking soda)
180ml (5¾fl oz) buttermilk

1 Preheat the oven to 160°C (315°F). Grease three 15cm (6 inch) round cake tins and line them with baking paper.

2 Place six slices of cooked satsuma at the bottom of each tin.

3 In a stand mixer with the whisk attachment, whisk the eggs and sugar on high speed until light and fluffy. While whisking, slowly pour the melted butter into the egg mixture and mix until combined. Add the vanilla bean paste and orange zest and mix to combine.

4 Sift one-quarter of the flour and one-quarter of the bicarbonate of soda over the mixture and gently fold them in using a spatula.

5 Add one-quarter of the buttermilk and mix well to combine.

6 Repeat steps 4 and 5 until all the flour mixture and buttermilk are used.

7 Divide the reserved satsuma slices among the tins, then spoon the batter evenly on top, levelling the surface. Bake for 25 minutes until a toothpick inserted into the cakes comes out clean. Leave to cool in the tins.

RAINBOW BUTTERCREAM

600g (1lb 5oz) unsalted butter,
   room temperature
600g (1lb 5oz) condensed milk
1 tablespoon vanilla bean paste
⅛ teaspoon each of red, orange,
   yellow, green, blue and purple
   gel food colouring

1   In a stand mixer with the paddle attachment, beat the butter until pale and creamy. While mixing, gradually add the condensed milk and mix to combine. Add the vanilla bean paste and mix until well combined.

2   Reserve two-thirds of the buttercream and leave it plain.

3   Divide the remaining buttercream evenly among six bowls and add a different food colouring to each. Mix until well combined and the colours are even.

TO ASSEMBLE

1   Prick the sponges with a toothpick, then drizzle the satsuma soak over them.

2   Place one sponge on a cake board or serving plate with the satsuma-soaked side up. Use one-quarter of the plain buttercream to cover the top of the cake.

3   Repeat to place the second sponge on top and cover with another one-quarter of the plain buttercream.

4   Top with the third sponge, then cover the top and side of the cake with the remaining plain buttercream, smoothing it out well with a cake scraper or palette knife.

5   Place the cake in the freezer for 30 minutes.

6   Remove from the freezer. Place a plastic stencil of a world map (with the map shape cut out of the plastic stencil) on the side of the cold cake.

7   To fill the template, use a small palette knife with a minimal amount of one of the purple buttercream to spread a stripe across the bottom of the world shape. Follow with a stripe of blue above the purple. Once all the colours have been applied in the order of the Pride flag (see photograph), carefully scrape off the excess buttercream with a cake scraper or spatula, then gently peel off the stencil.

8   Transfer the remaining coloured buttercreams to individual piping bags with star nozzles and pipe rosettes around the top of the cake.

9   Store in the fridge for up to 3 days. Serve at room temperature.

JANUSZ SAYS

When working with condensed milk buttercream make sure to mix it on a low speed or fold it with a spatula for about 2 minutes to get rid of any large air bubbles. This will create a much smoother texture and it will be easier to ice your cake super smoothly.

MAKES 30

Filled with colourful jams, these small, crisp, pastry parcels are the Polish equivalent of British jam tarts. They are easy to make and great to serve to guests along with a hot drink.

KOLACZKI WITH COLOURED JAMS

100g (3½oz) unsalted butter, room temperature

25g (1oz) icing (confectioners') sugar, sifted, plus extra to dust

100g (3½oz) cream cheese, room temperature

1 teaspoon vanilla bean paste

200g (7oz) plain (all-purpose) flour

150g (5½oz) colourful, fairly stiff, jams – such as strawberry, plum, apricot (a variety of colours is best, but you can use just one type of jam)

1 Grease two baking trays and line them with baking paper.

2 In a stand mixer with the paddle attachment, beat the butter and sugar until pale and creamy. Add the cream cheese and vanilla bean paste and mix to combine. Sift the flour over the mixture and mix until fully combined.

3 Wrap the pastry in plastic wrap and refrigerate for 1 hour.

4 On a floured work surface, roll out the pastry until 3mm (⅛ inch) thick.

5 Using a knife or cookie cutter, cut out 30 x 5cm (2 inch) squares.

6 Place roughly 1 teaspoon of jam in the middle of each square. Fold each square in half diagonally and seal the edges with a little water.

7 Transfer to the baking trays and refrigerate for 30 minutes.

8 Preheat the oven to 180°C (350°F).

9 Remove the trays from the fridge and bake for 15 minutes until golden brown. Cool on the tray for 5 minutes, then transfer to a wire rack to cool completely.

10 Once cool, dust with icing sugar and serve.

11 Store in an airtight container for up to 1 week.

MAKES 30

When I go home to Poland to visit my family, I look forward to eating my mother's homemade *pierniczki*, and I'm proud and excited to be sharing the recipe with you here. In this Polish classic a spicy gingerbread is stuffed with plum butter – the spices balancing beautifully with the sweet and sharp plum.

POLISH GINGERBREAD HEARTS IN RAINBOW COLOURS

DOUGH

80g (2¾oz) unsalted butter
110g (3¾oz) soft dark brown sugar
1 tablespoon ground cinnamon
1 teaspoon ground ginger
½ teaspoon ground cloves
½ teaspoon ground cardamom
¼ teaspoon ground allspice
¼ teaspoon ground nutmeg
pinch of black pepper
160g (5½oz) runny honey
1 large egg, room temperature
300g (10½oz) plain (all-purpose) flour
1 teaspoon bicarbonate of soda (baking soda)

PLUM BUTTER FILLING

300g (10½oz) plum butter (or grape butter)

DECORATION

100g (3½oz) white chocolate, chopped
1 teaspoon vegetable or coconut oil
red, orange, yellow, green, blue and purple gel food colouring

1. For the dough, combine the butter, sugar, spices and honey in a medium saucepan over medium heat and cook, whisking, until the sugar has dissolved.

2. Allow the mixture to cool until it is only slightly warm, then add the egg and whisk to combine.

3. Transfer the mixture to a stand mixer with the paddle attachment.

4. Sift the flour and bicarbonate of soda over the mixture and mix on low speed until you have a soft dough.

5. Wrap the dough in plastic wrap and refrigerate for 1 hour.

6. Remove the dough from the fridge. On a generously floured work surface, roll out the dough until 2–3mm (1⁄16 inch) thick.

7. Using a 7cm (2¾ inch) round cookie cutter, cut out 60 circles.

8. Grease two baking trays and line them with baking paper.

9. Place one circle of dough on the baking tray, add 1 teaspoon of plum butter in the centre of the circle, then place another dough circle on top.

10. Using a 7cm (2¾ inch) heart-shaped cookie cutter, cut a heart-shaped cookie out of the round cookie. Repeat to make 30 heart cookies.

11. Place the cookies on the trays and place in the freezer for 10 minutes.

12. Preheat the oven to 180°C (350°F).

13. Remove the cookies from the freezer and bake for 10 minutes until the edges are starting to brown. Cool slightly on the trays, then transfer to a wire rack to cool completely.

14. Heat the white chocolate with the oil in the microwave on High in 15-second bursts, stirring after each burst, until melted.

15. Divide the chocolate evenly among six bowls. Add three drops each of a different food colouring to each bowl and mix until well combined and the colours are even.

16. Dip the top surface of each heart cookie into one of the coloured chocolates.

17. Allow the chocolate to set before serving.

18. Store in an airtight container for up to 1 week.

JANUSZ SAYS

Plum butter is like jam with a very high fruit content and less sugar.

SERVES 8–10

This is probably the recipe I have been contacted most about on social media from people with Polish heritage. It is an old, traditional Polish bake, which every Polish person has had forced upon them by their *babcia* (grandmother). It consists of a deliciously airy, sweet, rolled pastry filled with a sweet poppy seed cream.

POLISH POPPY SEED ROULADE

DOUGH

160g (5½oz) plain (all-purpose) flour
70ml (2¼fl oz) full-cream (whole) milk, room temperature
2 large egg yolks, room temperature
7g (¼oz) active dried yeast
2 tablespoons soft dark brown sugar
2 teaspoons amaretto
1 teaspoon vanilla bean paste
pinch of salt

POPPY SEED FILLING

175g (6oz) poppy seeds
hot water
50g (1¾oz) soft light brown sugar
40g (1½oz) runny honey
30g (1oz) raisins
20g (¾oz) chopped pecans
1 teaspoon almond essence
1 tablespoon vanilla bean paste
½ teaspoon ground cinnamon
1 teaspoon unsalted butter, room temperature
60g (2¼oz) Italian cut mixed peel
2 large egg whites, room temperature

1   Combine all the dough ingredients in a stand mixer with the dough hook attachment and mix on medium speed for 10 minutes.

2   Cover the bowl with a clean tea towel (dish towel) and leave to prove in a warm place for 90 minutes.

3   Meanwhile, for the poppy seed filling, place the poppy seeds in a small saucepan and add hot water to cover. Cook over low heat for 15 minutes.

4   Preheat the oven to 190°C (375°F).

5   Strain the mixture through a piece of muslin (cheesecloth), squeezing the muslin to expel as much liquid as possible. Set aside to cool.

6   Once cool, squeeze out any excess water from the poppy seeds and blend them in a food processor for 1½ minutes, or until a paste forms.

7   In a large bowl, mix the blended poppy seeds with the soft light brown sugar, honey, raisins, chopped pecans, almond essence, vanilla bean paste, cinnamon, butter and Italian cut mixed peel.

8   In a separate bowl, use hand-held electric beaters to whisk the egg whites until stiff peaks form. Gently fold the egg whites into the poppy seed mixture using a spatula.

9   After the dough has risen, punch it down and knead it briefly on a floured work surface.

10 Roll out the dough into a 50 x 40cm (20 x 16 inch) rectangle, about 3mm (⅛ inch) thick.

TO ASSEMBLE

1 tablespoon water
150g (5½oz) icing
  (confectioners') sugar, sifted
50g (1¾oz) unsalted butter, room
  temperature
¼ teaspoon red gel food
  colouring
5g (⅛oz) poppy seeds

11 Spread the poppy seed filling over the dough, leaving a 2.5cm (1 inch) border around the edges.

12 Starting at a long edge, roll the dough into a sausage-shaped roulade, tucking the short ends underneath.

13 Cut a piece of baking paper large enough so you will be able to wrap it loosely around the roulade.

14 Wrap the baking paper around the roulade leaving a 1cm (½ inch) space between the paper and the roulade. Place the roulade on a baking tray lined with baking paper and bake for 35 minutes until golden brown.

15 While the roulade is still warm, whisk the water with 50g (1¾oz) of the icing sugar in a bowl, then brush this over the roulade.

16 Allow the roulade to cool completely on a wire rack.

17 In a stand mixer with the paddle attachment, beat the butter until pale and creamy. Add the remaining icing sugar and red food colouring and mix until combined and the colour is even.

18 Transfer the mixture to a piping bag with a petal nozzle and use it to pipe poppies on top of the roulade. Sprinkle poppy seeds inside the centre of the flowers.

19 Cut the roulade into thick slices to serve. Store in an airtight container for up to 3 days.

JANUSZ SAYS

Poppyseed cake, known as 'makowiec' in Poland, is a traditional Polish dessert often served during special occasions and holidays, particularly around Christmas and Easter.

MAKES 6

One of my favourite things about living in a seaside city is enjoying chips (fries) on the beach in summer. These white chocolate and salted crisp (potato chip) cupcakes, baked in newspaper print cases, are not only deliciously different, the sweet and salty cakes are a perfect representation of Brighton's fun, campy vibe.

'CHIPS ON THE BEACH' CUPCAKES

WHITE CHOCOLATE CUPCAKES

50g (1¾oz) unsalted butter
150g (5½oz) white chocolate, chopped into small pieces
pinch of salt
40g (1½oz) caster (superfine) sugar
1 large egg, room temperature
1 teaspoon natural vanilla extract
75g (2½oz) plain (all-purpose) flour
½ teaspoon baking powder

1   Preheat the oven to 180°C (350°F). Line six holes of a muffin tin with newspaper-print paper cases.

2   Combine the butter, 100g (3½oz) of the white chocolate and the salt in a small saucepan over medium heat and stir until the butter and chocolate are melted.

3   Remove the pan from the heat, add the sugar and whisk to combine. Leave to cool slightly, then add the egg and vanilla and mix well to combine. Sift the flour and baking powder over the mixture and stir until combined. Add the remaining chocolate and mix to combine.

4   Distribute the batter evenly between the holes in the muffin tin and bake for 15 minutes until golden. Cool for 10 minutes in the tin, then transfer to a wire rack to cool completely.

WHITE CHOCOLATE BUTTERCREAM

60g (2¼oz) white chocolate, chopped
60g (2¼oz) unsalted butter, room temperature
60g (2¼oz) icing (confectioners') sugar, sifted

1   Heat the chocolate in the microwave on High in 20-second bursts, stirring after each burst, until melted. Allow to cool but not set.

2   Using hand-held electric beaters, whisk the butter until pale and creamy. While whisking, add the sugar, a teaspoon at a time, and mix until fully incorporated. Add the melted chocolate and whisk for a few seconds until combined.

TO ASSEMBLE

25g (1oz) ready salted crinkle cut crisps (potato chips), crushed
chip forks

1   Put the crushed potato chips in a bowl.

2   Roughly spread the buttercream on top of the cupcakes and form a peak at the top.

3   Turn the cupcakes upside down and dip the peak of buttercream into the bowl of crushed potato chips. Top the cupcake with a chip fork stuck into the top at an angle.

4   Store in an airtight container for up to 3 days.

Living in the UK, I love being able to travel to places that are home to classic bakes, from Cornish pasties to Scottish shortbread. Inspired by my own trip to Bakewell in Derbyshire, my Pride-decorated bakewell tarts have a shortcrust pastry case filled with jam and frangipane and are topped with feathered rainbow Pride icing.

RAINBOW MINI BAKEWELL TARTS

SHORTCRUST PASTRY

60g (2¼oz) unsalted butter, cold, cubed
50g (1¾oz) icing (confectioners') sugar, sifted
120g (4¼oz) plain (all-purpose) flour, sifted
1 teaspoon vanilla bean paste
1 egg yolk, room temperature
pinch of salt

RASPBERRY FILLING

2 tablespoons seedless raspberry jam
6 raspberries, cut in half lengthways
2 large eggs, room temperature
75g (2½oz) caster (superfine) sugar
75g (2½oz) almond meal
70g (2½oz) unsalted butter, melted and cooled
½ teaspoon almond essence

ICING

150g (5½oz) icing (confectioners') sugar, sifted
3–4 tablespoons hot water
½ teaspoon almond essence
red, orange, yellow, green, blue and purple gel food colouring

1. Grease six 10cm (4 inch) flan (tart) tins.

2. For the pastry, in a stand mixer with the paddle attachment, mix the butter, icing sugar and flour on low speed until the texture resembles breadcrumbs. Add the vanilla bean paste, egg yolk and salt and mix until a smooth dough forms.

3. Wrap the dough in plastic wrap and refrigerate for 30 minutes. Remove the dough from the fridge and let it rest for 5 minutes.

4. Divide the dough into six equal portions and roll them into balls. On a floured work surface, roll each ball out to fit the tart tins.

5. Drape a pastry circle over your rolling pin and lower it into the tin, pressing the pastry into the tin with your fingers. Trim off any excess pastry. Once all the tins are lined with pastry, freeze them for 20 minutes.

6. Preheat the oven to 180°C (350°F).

7. Remove the tins from the freezer. Cover the pastry with baking paper, fill with baking beans and bake for 10 minutes. Remove from the oven, take out the beans and paper, then bake for a further 3 minutes until golden brown. Allow to cool to room temperature in the tins.

8. For the filling, spread 1 teaspoon of jam in the bottom of each tart. Place the raspberry halves in the bottom of each tart.

9. Blitz the eggs, sugar and almond meal in a food processor until the texture is like a gritty custard. While blitzing, slowly pour the melted butter and almond essence into the food processor and mix to combine.

10. Divide the filling evenly among the tartlets and bake for 15 minutes. Remove from the oven and let them cool to room temperature in the tins. Remove the tarts from the tins.

11. For the icing, mix the icing sugar with the hot water and almond essence in a small bowl until combined.

12. Remove six 2-teaspoon amounts of the icing and place them in separate small bowls. Add three drops each of a different food colouring to each bowl and mix until each portion is an even colour.

13. Transfer the white icing to a disposable piping bag with one corner cut off, and the coloured icing to separate piping bags with small plain nozzles. Working on one tart at a time, cover the top with white icing.

14. Draw thin lines across the tart with the coloured icings. Using a toothpick, create a feathered effect by moving the toothpick backwards and forwards through the coloured stripes (see photograph). Repeat to ice the other tarts, then leave to set for 1 hour before serving.

15. Store in an airtight container for up to 3 days.

MAKES 18

These cute, camp madeleines consist of a light, airy blue and pink sponge, and are dipped in white chocolate and then topped with sprinkles and edible pearls. While visually dramatic, the madeleines retain the traditional flavour and consistency that makes them so universally adored.

mermaID TaIL maDeLeInes

2 large eggs, room temperature
2 pinches of salt
blue and pink gel food colouring
1 teaspoon vanilla bean paste
110g (3¾oz) caster (superfine)
  sugar
100g (3½oz) plain (all-purpose)
  flour
½ teaspoon baking powder
100g (3½oz) unsalted butter,
  melted and cooled
60g (2¼oz) white chocolate,
  chopped
10g (⅓oz) small edible pearls
20g (¾oz) luxury sprinkles – the
  ones I buy online are called
  'Edible Fizz Pop Decorations'
  and are pink, purple, silver and
  white

1 In a stand mixer with the whisk attachment, whisk one egg, the salt, three drops of blue food colouring, half the vanilla bean paste and half the sugar on high speed until light and fluffy.

2 Sift half the flour and half the baking powder over the mixture and fold them in gently using a spatula.

3 Evenly distribute half of the cooled melted butter into the batter and fold it in gently.

4 In a separate bowl, repeat steps 1–3 with the remaining ingredients, adding three drops of pink food colouring this time.

5 Transfer the coloured batters, a tablespoon at a time, to a bowl, then gently move a teaspoon backwards and forwards through the mixture to achieve a marbled effect.

6 Cover the bowl with plastic wrap and refrigerate for 60 minutes.

7 Preheat the oven to 175°C (345°F).

8 Grease and flour an 18-hole madeleine tin, shake off the excess flour and refrigerate for 15 minutes.

9 Remove the batter from the fridge. Add 1 tablespoon of batter to each madeleine mould and bake for 9 minutes. Remove from the oven and set aside to cool in the tin for 5 minutes.

10 Remove the madeleines from the tin and transfer to a wire rack to cool completely.

11 Heat the white chocolate in the microwave on High in 30-second bursts, stirring after each burst, until melted.

12 Dip the wide end of the madeleines into the melted chocolate at an angle to create a neat diagonal line, then dip again in the opposite direction so you are left with a V shape (see photograph). Transfer to a wire rack with a sheet of baking paper underneath to catch any drips.

13 Using a teaspoon, sprinkle the edible pearls and sprinkles across the chocolate-coated ends of the madeleines and leave to set before serving.

14 Store in an airtight container for up to 3 days.

These smooth, seashell-themed macarons are inspired by my new home by the beach in Brighton. The flavours are a perfect complement of lime and coconut and anyone who tastes them will immediately reminisce about times by the sea.

seasHell macarons

MACARONS

100g (3½oz) almond meal
90g (3¼oz) icing (confectioners') sugar
80g (2¾oz) egg whites, room temperature
90g (3¼oz) caster (superfine) sugar

1 Preheat the oven to 120°C (235°F). Grease a baking tray and line it with baking paper.

2 Blitz the almond meal and icing sugar in a food processor for 10 seconds. Shake the food processor, then blitz for a further 5 seconds. Sift the mixture into a bowl.

3 In a stand mixer with the whisk attachment, whisk the egg whites until stiff peaks form. While whisking, gradually add the caster sugar, a tablespoon at a time, until fully incorporated. Add one-quarter of the almond mixture and mix to combine. Gently fold in the remaining almond mixture using a spatula.

4 Transfer the mixture to a piping bag with a plain nozzle.

5 Pipe five strips of the mixture onto the tray, with the strips butting up against each other, to form the shape of a scallop-style seashell – use two short strips on the outside, two slightly longer ones inside those and an even longer strip in the middle.

6 Bake for 16 minutes until the top of the macarons is hard to the touch and the surface is smooth and glossy. Leave to cool on the tray.

COCONUT WHITE CHOCOLATE GANACHE

50g (1¾oz) coconut cream
150g (5½oz) white chocolate, chopped

1 Heat the coconut cream in a saucepan over medium–high heat until almost boiling.

2 Remove the pan from the heat. Add the chocolate and leave to sit for 2 minutes, then stir until the chocolate is melted and the mixture is smooth.

3 Leave the chocolate to set to a pipeable consistency.

4 Transfer the ganache to a piping bag with a star nozzle.

LIME CURD

zest and juice of 2 limes
3 egg yolks, room temperature
30g (1oz) unsalted butter
60g (2¼oz) caster (superfine) sugar

1 Combine all the ingredients in a saucepan over medium heat and bring to the boil, stirring constantly.

2 Remove the pan from the heat and set aside to cool.

3 Transfer to a piping bag with a small plain nozzle.

TO ASSEMBLE

1. Pipe a circle of white chocolate ganache on top of a macaron, leaving a hole in the centre.

2. Fill the centre of the circle with lime curd and top with a second macaron.

3. Serve the macarons with the remaining lime curd as a dip.

4. Store in an airtight container for up to 7 days.

This sweet vanilla sponge cake has a deliciously sharp rhubarb filling and is topped with colourful icing in the shape of a rainbow. Rhubarb is a popular flavour in my home country, Poland, as well as my second home, the UK.

RHUBARB CaKe

RHUBARB FILLING

600g (1lb 5oz) rhubarb (forced rhubarb is best), chopped
150g (5½oz) caster (superfine) sugar
2 tablespoons lemon juice
35g (1¼oz) cornflour (cornstarch)
3 tablespoons water

1 Combine the rhubarb, sugar and lemon juice in a saucepan over medium–high heat and cook for 1–2 minutes until the rhubarb becomes soft, but not mushy.

2 In a separate bowl, mix the cornflour with the water to form a paste.

3 Add the cornflour mixture to the pan with the rhubarb and cook for 1 minute more, stirring constantly. Remove from the heat and set aside.

VANILLA SPONGE

3 large eggs, room temperature
120g (4¼oz) icing (confectioners') sugar, sifted
1 teaspoon vanilla bean paste
100ml (3½fl oz) vegetable oil
2 tablespoons buttermilk
150g (5½oz) plain (all-purpose) flour
½ teaspoon baking powder

1 Preheat the oven to 180°C (350°F). Line the base and sides of a deep 20cm (8 inch) square cake tin with baking paper.

2 In a stand mixer with the whisk attachment, whisk the eggs, sugar and vanilla bean paste until fluffy. Add the oil and buttermilk and mix until well combined. Sift the flour and baking powder over the mixture and fold them in using a spatula.

3 Pour half the batter into the tin, level the surface, then bake for 15 minutes.

4 Remove from the oven. Pour the rhubarb mixture over the baked cake in the tin and level the surface.

5 Pour the remaining cake batter on top of the rhubarb layer and level the surface. Bake for a further 25 minutes until the top of the cake springs back when pressed with a finger.

6 Allow the cake to cool completely in the tin.

RAINBOW ICING

140g (5oz) icing (confectioners') sugar, sifted
3–4 tablespoons hot water
red, orange, yellow, green, blue and purple food colouring

1. In a small bowl, mix the icing sugar with the hot water until it is a thick but pourable consistency.

2. Reserve 2 tablespoons of the icing mixture, then divide the remaining icing evenly among six bowls. Add one drop of a different food colouring to each bowl and mix until each portion is an even colour.

3. Transfer each coloured icing into separate piping bags with small plain nozzles.

TO ASSEMBLE

1. Invert the cake onto a serving plate and peel off the baking paper.

2. Pipe the rainbow in the middle of the cake with the coloured icing. Fill the uncovered areas of the cake with white icing.

3. Allow the icing to set before cutting into nine squares and serving.

4. Store in an airtight container for up to 3 days.

JANUSZ SAYS

'Forced' rhubarb is rhubarb that is woken from its winter nap early so it doesn't develop a green tint or large leaves. It has a delicate and much sweeter flavour, and is more tender than regular rhubarb.

BRUNCH
BAKES

SERVES 12

This fun, quirky tray bake is the perfect brunch pudding and was one of my favourite sweets growing up in Poland. It has a layer of light lemon and poppy seed sponge, a layer of sweet vanilla cheesecake and is topped with apricots to look like fried eggs.

FRIED EGG ILLUSION TRAY BAKE

LEMON & POPPY SEED SPONGE

1 large egg, room temperature
120g (4¼oz) caster (superfine) sugar
60ml (2fl oz) vegetable oil
1 tablespoon natural vanilla extract
zest of 1 large lemon
180g (6½oz) plain (all-purpose) flour
1 teaspoon baking powder
½ teaspoon bicarbonate of soda (baking soda)
¼ teaspoon salt
25g (1oz) poppy seeds
125ml (4fl oz) buttermilk

1 Preheat the oven to 350°F (175°C). Grease a 35 x 24 x 5cm (14 x 9½ x 2 inch) baking tin and line it with baking paper.

2 In a stand mixer with the whisk attachment, whisk the egg and sugar until light and fluffy. Add the oil, vanilla and lemon zest and whisk until combined.

3 Sift the flour, baking powder, bicarbonate of soda and salt into a separate bowl and add the poppy seeds. Stir to combine.

4 While whisking, gradually add the dry ingredients to the wet mixture, alternating with the buttermilk, and mix until combined.

5 Pour the batter into the tin, level the surface and bake for 20 minutes until a toothpick inserted into the cake comes out clean.

VANILLA CHEESECAKE FILLING

5 platinum gelatine leaves
150ml (5fl oz) water
juice and zest of 2 lemons (around 100ml/3½fl oz lemon juice)
150g (5½oz) granulated sugar
400g (14oz) cream cheese, room temperature
400g (14oz) mascarpone
150g (5½oz) icing (confectioners') sugar, sifted
200g (7oz) double (thick) cream
2 x 420g (15oz) tins of apricot halves in syrup (syrup reserved) – you will need 12 halves

1 Soak the gelatine in cold water for 5 minutes until softened.

2 Combine the water, lemon juice, lemon zest and sugar in a medium saucepan over medium heat and bring to the boil. Cook, stirring, until the sugar has completely dissolved and the liquid has reduced to about 200ml (7fl oz) – about 10 minutes.

3 Remove the saucepan from the heat. Squeeze the excess water from the gelatine and add the gelatine to the pan, stirring until it is dissolved.

4 Pass the mixture through a fine-mesh sieve into a bowl to remove any lemon zest. Set aside at room temperature to thicken but not set.

5 In a stand mixer with the whisk attachment, whip the cream cheese, mascarpone and icing sugar until smooth. Add the cream and whisk until the mixture has thickened. Add the thickened jelly and mix until combined.

6 Pour the cheesecake mixture on top of the cake in the tin and level the surface.

7 Place the apricot halves, cut side down, on top of the cheese mixture, gently pressing them in so the visible part is the size of an egg yolk.

8 Refrigerate for 2 hours until the cheesecake has set.

JELLY TOP
500ml (17fl oz) reserved apricot
  syrup
4 platinum gelatine leaves

1 Pour a few tablespoons of the apricot syrup over the gelatine in a bowl – just enough to cover – and soak for 10 minutes.

2 Heat the remaining syrup in a saucepan over medium heat until almost boiling. Squeeze the liquid out of the gelatine and add the gelatine to the pan, stirring until it is dissolved.

3 Set the jelly mixture aside to cool and thicken slightly, but not set.

4 Pour the jelly mixture over the cheesecake until everything is covered.

5 Refrigerate for at least 4 hours before slicing and serving. When you cut the cake, ensure each slice has an apricot positioned in the centre to look like a fried egg.

6 Store in an airtight container in the fridge for up to 4 days.

JANUSZ SAYS

For an additional touch of brunch vibes, thinly slice some pistachios to garnish the top of the apricots. Now you have fried eggs with chives!

MAKES 6

This bake holds a special place in my heart as it brings back memories of lazy Saturday mornings when all I needed to make everything all right was a warm, freshly baked *rogaliki* dipped in a cup of cocoa. The soft and buttery texture of these croissants, combined with the sweet chocolate spread and vibrant sprinkles, makes them an absolute delight to indulge in.

ROGALIKI – POLISH CROISSANTS

300g (10½oz) strong flour, sifted
200ml (7fl oz) full-cream (whole) milk
7g (¼oz) active dried yeast
3 tablespoons caster (superfine) sugar)
40g (1½oz) unsalted butter, melted and cooled
pinch of salt
6 tablespoons chocolate hazelnut spread
1 tablespoon rainbow sprinkles

1   In a stand mixer with the dough hook attachment, mix the flour, milk, yeast and sugar for 5 minutes on medium speed until a dough forms. Add the melted butter and salt and knead for a further 3–5 minutes.

2   Cover the bowl with plastic wrap and leave the dough to prove in a warm place for 90 minutes until doubled in size.

3   Grease a large baking tray and line it with baking paper.

4   Punch the dough down and knead it briefly on a floured work surface.

5   Divide the dough into six equal portions. Roll each portion into a long oval, about 50cm (20 inches) in length.

6   Place 1 tablespoon of chocolate hazelnut spread along one short end of the dough and roll the end of the dough over the spread and seal – this helps prevent the spread from leaking out during baking.

7   Scatter the sprinkles evenly over the dough.

8   Starting at the end with the pocket of spread, use your hand to roll the oval of dough into a cylinder.

9   Bend the cylinder into a crescent and place it on the baking tray. Repeat the process with the remaining five pieces of dough.

10 Leave the croissants in a warm place to prove for 30 minutes, covered with a clean tea towel (dish towel).

11 Preheat the oven to 200°C (400°F).

12 Bake the croissants for 15 minutes until golden brown. Serve warm or transfer to a wire rack to cool.

13 The croissants are best eaten on the day they are made, but can be stored in an airtight container for up to 2 days.

SERVES 6

This rich, creamy mocha pudding, topped with poached meringue and a heart-shaped sugar cookie, is the perfect finale to a fun brunch with friends.

MOCHA PUDDING WITH POACHED MERINGUES

POACHED MERINGUES

3 large egg whites, room temperature
125g (4½oz) caster (superfine) sugar
250g (9oz) double (thick) cream
250ml (9fl oz) full-cream (whole) milk

1 In a stand mixer with the whisk attachment, whisk the egg whites until stiff peaks form. While whisking, gradually add the sugar, a tablespoon at a time, until fully incorporated. Transfer the mixture to a piping bag with a star nozzle.

2 Prepare six squares of baking paper the same width as your serving mugs. Pipe a decorative swirl of meringue (see photograph) that is 1cm (½ inch) smaller than the diameter of your serving mugs onto the squares of baking paper.

3 Combine the cream and milk in a large saucepan over medium heat and bring almost to the boil.

4 Reduce the heat to low and carefully transfer your piped meringues, still on the baking paper, into the saucepan. Cover and steam for 5 minutes, making sure the milk does not boil.

5 Once cooked, transfer the meringues to a wire rack to cool.

MOCHA CRÈME ANGLAISE

225ml (7¾fl oz) full-cream (whole) milk
250g (9oz) double (thick) cream
6 large eggs yolks, room temperature
60g (2¼oz) caster (superfine) sugar
1½ tablespoons freshly prepared espresso coffee
20g (¾oz) dark chocolate (70% cocoa solids), chopped

1 Combine the milk and cream in a medium saucepan over medium heat and bring almost to the boil.

2 In a large bowl, using hand-held electric beaters, whisk the egg yolks and sugar until light and fluffy. Whisking constantly, add half the hot milk and cream mixture to the egg yolk and whisk until fully combined.

3 Transfer the mixture to the pan with the remaining hot milk and cream and stir in the coffee.

4 Whisk until the mixture thickens, making sure it does not boil.

5 Add the chocolate to the saucepan and mix until melted and combined.

SUGAR COOKIES

50g (1¾oz) unsalted butter, cold, cubed
75g (2½oz) plain (all-purpose) flour
1 egg yolk, room temperature
25g (1oz) icing (confectioners') sugar
¼ teaspoon red gel food colouring

1 Preheat the oven to 190°C (375°F). Grease a baking tray and line it with baking paper.

2 Place all the ingredients in a food processor and blitz until the texture resembles breadcrumbs.

3 On a floured work surface, knead the mixture into a dough. Roll out the dough until 5mm (¼ inch) thick.

4 Using a 5cm (2 inch) heart-shaped cookie cutter, cut out six cookies and place them on the baking tray.

5 Place in the freezer for 10 minutes.

6 Remove from the freezer and bake for 7 minutes until slightly golden. Set aside to cool on the tray for 5 minutes, then transfer to a wire rack to cool completely.

TO ASSEMBLE

½ teaspoon pure unsweetened
  cocoa powder, sifted

1 Warm the crème anglaise and divide
   between six 150ml (5fl oz) mugs –
   use glass mugs for the best effect.

2 Peel the baking paper off the
   poached meringues and place one
   on top of each mug, then top with a
   sugar cookie. Dust with the cocoa
   and serve immediately.

MAKES 6

These sweet tacos consist of a thin, vanilla sponge, folded and filled with whipped orange sweet cream and fresh strawberries, then dusted with icing sugar to finish.

SWEET TACOS

TACOS
3 large eggs, room temperature, separated
pinch of salt
50g (1¾oz) caster (superfine) sugar
1½ teaspoons vanilla bean paste
40g (1½oz) plain (all-purpose) flour
10g (⅓oz) cornflour (cornstarch)
icing (confectioners') sugar, to dust

ORANGE CREAM
600g (1 lb 5oz) double (thick) cream
50g (1¾oz) icing (confectioners') sugar, sifted
2 teaspoons vanilla bean paste
1 teaspoon grated orange zest

TO ASSEMBLE
12 large fresh strawberries, sliced, to decorate
icing (confectioners') sugar, to dust

1 Preheat the oven to 180°C (350°F).

2 Prepare two sheets of baking paper that will fit the length of a baking tray. Draw three 12cm (4½ inch) circles on each sheet. Make the circles dark enough so you can see the circles through the paper, then place the sheets of paper upside down on two baking trays.

3 In a stand mixer with the whisk attachment, whisk the egg whites until slightly frothy. Add the salt and whisk until stiff peaks form.

4 While whisking, gradually add the caster sugar, a tablespoon at a time, until fully incorporated. Add the egg yolks, one at a time, mixing after each addition. Add the vanilla bean paste and whisk until combined.

5 Sift the flour and cornflour over the mixture and fold them in gently using a spatula, forming a light batter.

6 Spread 2 heaped tablespoons of batter evenly within the outlines of the six circles on the baking paper. Bake for 6 minutes until lightly golden.

7 Remove from the oven and immediately and carefully peel the six sponges off the baking paper.

8 Place the sponges, top down, on a clean tea towel (dish towel) dusted with icing sugar.

9 Use the tea towel to fold the circles in half, then set aside to cool inside the tea towel.

10 For the orange cream, in a stand mixer with the whisk attachment, whip the cream, sugar, vanilla and orange zest until soft peaks form.

11 Transfer to a piping bag with a large star nozzle.

12 Remove the folded sponge 'tacos' from the tea towel and place on a serving plate.

13 Pipe the cream evenly inside the folded sponges and top with sliced strawberries. Dust the tops with icing sugar before serving.

14 Store in an airtight container in the fridge for 24 hours.

MAKES 6

These cake jars contain alternating layers of moist vanilla sponge and banana and raspberry cream. They taste so indulgent, you wouldn't think fresh fruit could taste this decadent! The colours of the mousse represent the colours of the transgender Pride flag – light blue, pink and white.

RASPBERRY BANANA TRANS CAKE JARS

VANILLA SPONGE

3 large eggs, room temperature
225g (8oz) caster (superfine) sugar
125ml (4fl oz) vegetable oil
1 tablespoon vanilla bean paste
225g (8oz) plain (all-purpose) flour
1 teaspoon baking powder
1 teaspoon bicarbonate of soda (baking soda)
180ml (5¾fl oz) buttermilk

1   Preheat the oven to 180°C (350°F). Line a 35 x 24 x 5cm (14 x 9½ x 2 inch) baking tin with baking paper.

2   In a stand mixer with the whisk attachment, whisk the eggs and sugar on high speed until light and fluffy. While whisking, slowly pour in the oil and vanilla bean paste and mix to combine.

3   In a separate bowl, mix together the flour, baking powder and bicarbonate of soda.

4   Sift half of the flour mixture over the wet ingredients and fold it in using a spatula.

5   Add half of the buttermilk and fold it in.

6   Add the remaining flour mixture and fold it in.

7   Add the remaining buttermilk and fold it in using a spatula.

8   Transfer the batter to the prepared baking tin and bake for 25 minutes until a toothpick inserted into the cake comes out clean. Leave to cool in the tin.

BANANA CREAM

200g (7oz) bananas, cut into small pieces
400ml (14fl oz) full-cream (whole) milk
½ teaspoon banana essence
4 egg yolks, room temperature
40g (1½oz) plain (all-purpose) flour, sifted
60g (2¼oz) caster (superfine) sugar
3 drops of white gel food colouring
⅛ teaspoon blue gel food colouring
2 platinum gelatine leaves
100ml (3½fl oz) water
300g (10½oz) double (thick) cream

1   In a food processor or blender, blitz the bananas with the milk and banana essence until smooth.

2   In a large bowl, using hand-held electric beaters, whisk the egg yolks, flour and sugar until smooth.

3   Heat the banana mixture in a saucepan over medium heat, stirring constantly, until almost boiling.

4   Whisk the hot banana milk into the bowl with the egg yolks until well combined. Pass the mixture through a fine-mesh sieve, then return to the pan over medium heat. Bring to the boil, then remove from the heat. Cover with plastic wrap touching the surface of the mixture, to prevent a skin forming, then chill in the fridge for at least 1 hour.

5   Remove from the fridge. Whisk the mixture until smooth and divide it evenly between two bowls. Add white food colouring to one bowl and blue to the other. Mix until well combined and the colours are even.

6   Soak the gelatine in the water for 10 minutes. Squeeze the excess water from the gelatine, then melt the gelatine in the microwave on High for up to 5 seconds.

7   In a stand mixer with the whisk attachment, whip the cream until soft peaks form. Add the gelatine and whip until thickened and the gelatine is dissolved. Divide the cream evenly between the two bowls of banana mixture and fold it in. Transfer each to a piping bag with a plain nozzle and refrigerate until needed.

RASPBERRY CREAM

100g (3½oz) raspberries
200ml (7fl oz) full-cream
  (whole) milk
2 egg yolks, room temperature
40g (1½oz) caster (superfine)
  sugar
20g (¾oz) plain (all-purpose) flour,
  sifted
1 drop of pink gel food colouring
1 platinum gelatine leaf
50ml (1½fl oz) water
150g (5½oz) double (thick) cream

1. In a food processor or blender, blitz the raspberries with the milk until smooth.

2. In a large bowl, combine the egg yolks, sugar, flour and food colouring and mix until smooth.

3. Heat the raspberry milk mixture in a saucepan over medium heat, stirring occasionally, until almost boiling.

4. Whisk the hot raspberry milk into the bowl with the egg yolks until well combined.

5. Pass the mixture through a fine-mesh sieve, then return to the pan over medium heat. Bring to the boil, then remove from the heat.

6. Cover with plastic wrap touching the surface of the mixture, to prevent a skin forming, then chill in the fridge for about 1 hour.

7. Remove from the fridge. Using hand-held electric beaters, whisk until smooth.

8. Soak the gelatine in the water for 10 minutes.

9. Squeeze the excess water from the gelatine, then melt the gelatine in the microwave on High for up to 5 seconds.

10. In a stand mixer with the whisk attachment, whip the cream until soft peaks form. Add the gelatine and whip until thickened and the gelatine is dissolved.

11. Fold the cream into the raspberry mixture.

12. Transfer to a piping bag with a plain nozzle and refrigerate until needed.

TO ASSEMBLE

1. Cut nine circles out of the sponge cake to fit inside your jars. (I use 370ml/12¾fl oz jars.) Set the cake scraps aside. Cut each sponge circle in half, horizontally, so you have two thinner circles (18 circles in total).

2. Place a circle of cake in the bottom of the jars and crumble in some of the left-over cake scraps.

3. Pipe a layer of white banana cream into each jar, then top with another sponge circle and add more cake crumbs.

4. Pipe a layer of blue banana cream into each jar, then top with another sponge circle and cake crumbs.

5. Pipe a layer of raspberry cream into each jar.

6. Store in an airtight container in the fridge for up to 2 days.

Serve your guests some magic with these pastry unicorn horns dipped in white chocolate and filled with a deliciously tart strawberry cream.

HNICORN PASTRY HORNS

STRAWBERRY CREAM FILLING

3 platinum gelatine leaves
100ml (3½fl oz) water
200g (7oz) frozen strawberries
50g (1¾oz) caster (superfine) sugar
juice of ½ lemon
100g (3½oz) mascarpone
125g (4½oz) double (thick) cream

1 Soak the gelatine in the water for 10 minutes.

2 Place the strawberries, sugar and lemon juice in a small saucepan over high heat and cook for about 10 minutes until the strawberries have softened.

3 Transfer the mixture to a food processor or blender and blitz to a purée.

4 Squeeze the excess water from the gelatine and add the gelatine to the hot strawberry mixture. Stir until combined, then set aside to cool, but not set.

5 In a stand mixer with the whisk attachment, whip the mascarpone and cream until soft peaks form.

6 While mixing on low speed, gradually add the strawberry mixture and mix until well combined.

7 Cover the mixture with plastic wrap touching the surface, to prevent a skin forming, then refrigerate for 6 hours.

Unicorns are real!

PASTRY HORNS

125g (4½oz) unsalted butter,
  chilled and cubed
125g (4½oz) strong flour, sifted
¼ teaspoon salt
75ml (2¼fl oz) iced water
3 drops of pink gel food colouring
12 metal pastry cones 12 x 3cm
  (4½ x 1¼ inches)

1   Place the butter, flour and salt
    in a stand mixer with the paddle
    attachment. Mix on low speed for
    a couple of turns, just until the butter
    is covered with flour.

2   In a small bowl, combine the water
    and food colouring.

3   While mixing on low speed, add the
    coloured water to the butter and
    flour mixture and mix until a dough
    forms with visible lumps of butter
    still present.

4   Transfer the dough to a generously
    floured work surface and roll it
    out into a 40 x 20cm (16 x 8 inch)
    rectangle.

5   Fold the short sides of the rectangle
    into the centre. Turn the dough
    90 degrees, then fold in half.

6   Repeat steps 4 and 5.

7   Wrap the dough in plastic wrap
    and transfer it to the freezer for
    15 minutes.

8   Repeat steps 4–7 twice more to
    achieve a laminated pastry dough.

9   Remove the dough from the
    freezer. On a floured work surface,
    roll the dough out into a 60 x 24cm
    (24 x 9½ inch) rectangle.

10 Cut 12 strips of dough, 60cm
    (24 inches) long and 2cm (¾ inch)
    wide.

11 Wrap the strips of pastry around
    the metal pastry cones in a spiral,
    working from the wide to the narrow
    end. Pinch the end of the dough so
    that it doesn't unravel during baking.

12 Refrigerate the moulds for
    30 minutes.

13 Preheat the oven to 180°C (350°F).

14 Remove the cones from the fridge
    and bake for 20 minutes until puffed
    and crisp and the edges are a deep
    golden brown. Transfer to a wire rack
    and remove the metal cone when the
    horns are completely cool.

TO ASSEMBLE

50g (1¾oz) white chocolate,
  chopped
rainbow sprinkles

1   Heat the white chocolate in the
    microwave on High in 15-second
    bursts, stirring after each burst,
    until melted.

2   Place the sprinkles in a bowl.

3   Dip the open end of each horn in
    the white chocolate, then dip the
    chocolate into the bowl of sprinkles
    to cover. Leave on a wire rack to set.

4   Remove the strawberry cream
    mixture from the fridge and transfer
    to a large piping bag with a star
    nozzle.

5   Place the nozzle into a pastry horn
    and pipe in the strawberry cream
    until some extends out of the end to
    resemble an ice cream cone.

6   The unfilled pastry horns can be
    stored in an airtight container for
    up to 3 days. The cream can be
    stored in an airtight container in
    the fridge for up to 2 days. Pipe the
    cream just before serving.

SERVES 8–10

As an avid cereal fan, this is my favourite recipe in the book. The sweet cereal milk tart has a sprinkle-coloured shortcrust pastry casing filled with a wholegrain cereal-infused milk pudding, and is topped with whipped cream and colourful cereal marshmallows.

BREAKFAST CEREAL MILK TART

SHORTCRUST PASTRY

90g (3¼oz) unsalted butter, cold, cubed
140g (5oz) plain (all-purpose) flour, sifted
30g (1oz) icing (confectioners') sugar, sifted
1 teaspoon vanilla bean paste
1 large egg yolk, room temperature
40g (1½oz) rainbow sprinkles

1. In a stand mixer with the paddle attachment, mix the butter, flour and sugar on low speed until the texture resembles breadcrumbs. Add the vanilla bean paste and egg yolk and mix until a smooth dough forms.

2. Add the sprinkles and fold them in using a spatula.

3. Wrap the dough in plastic wrap and refrigerate for 30 minutes.

4. Remove the dough from the fridge and leave to stand for 5 minutes.

5. On a floured work surface, roll out the dough to fit into a 19cm (7½ inch) round flan (tart) tin.

6. Line the tin with the dough and place in the freezer for 30 minutes.

7. Preheat the oven to 180°C (350°F).

8. Remove the pastry from the freezer. Cover the pastry with baking paper, fill with baking beans and bake for 15 minutes.

9. Remove from the oven and remove the beans and paper. Return the tart case to the oven to bake for a further 10 minutes until golden. Leave to cool in the tin.

MILK PUDDING

200g (7oz) Lucky Charms/ Marshmallow Mateys cereal (sugar-frosted wholegrain oat cereal containing colourful mini marshmallow charms)
4 tablespoons caster (superfine) sugar
500ml (17fl oz) full-cream (whole) milk
250g (9oz) double (thick) cream
3 platinum gelatine leaves
100ml (3½fl oz) water
1 tablespoon cornflour (cornstarch)

1. Remove the marshmallow charms from the cereal and save them for decorating the tart.

2. Place the cereal, sugar, milk and cream in a saucepan over medium–high heat and bring to the boil.

3. Remove the pan from the heat and set aside for 1 hour.

4. Sieve the milk mixture and discard the cereal – you should have around 450ml (16fl oz) of liquid left.

5. Soak the gelatine in the water for 10 minutes.

6. Place the milk in a saucepan. Add the cornflour and whisk to combine. Set the pan over medium heat and bring to the boil, whisking constantly.

7. Remove the pan from the heat. Squeeze the excess water out of the gelatine and add the gelatine to the pan, stirring until dissolved. Leave the mixture to cool to room temperature.

8. Transfer the mixture to the fridge, checking every 5 minutes to see if it is starting to set.

9. Once it starts to set, pour the mixture into the pastry shell and refrigerate for 1 hour until fully set. Remove the tart from the tin and place on a serving plate.

TO ASSEMBLE

300g (10½oz) double (thick)
  cream
30g (1oz) icing (confectioners')
  sugar, sifted
1 teaspoon vanilla bean paste
reserved marshmallow charms
  from the cereal

1 In a stand mixer with the whisk
   attachment, whip the cream, sugar
   and vanilla bean paste until soft
   peaks form. Transfer the mixture to
   a piping bag with a plain nozzle and,
   starting in the centre, pipe a spiral of
   cream on top of the tart to cover it.

2 Place the marshmallow charms
   around the edge of the tart.

3 Serve chilled. Store in the fridge
   for up to 8 days.

SERVES 4

Here's something different to serve your brunch guests. This waffle tower cake is constructed from a stack of four light, tasty waffles filled with whipped cream, fresh fruit and a dash of maple syrup. It should be sliced and served with love – with no mention of calories.

WAFFLE TOWER CAKE

2 large eggs, separated, room temperature
2 tablespoons vegetable oil
250ml (9fl oz) buttermilk
¾ teaspoon baking powder, sifted
120g (4¼oz) plain (all-purpose) flour, sifted
pinch of salt
1 tablespoon caster (superfine) sugar
400g (14oz) double (thick) cream
50g (1¾oz) icing (confectioners') sugar
8–9 fresh strawberries, sliced, plus 6–8 more halved or whole with their stems on, to decorate
15 fresh raspberries
2 kiwi fruit, peeled and chopped
100g (3½oz) fresh blueberries
50g (1¾oz) pomegranate seeds
100g (3½oz) orange segments (no skin or pith)
160ml (5¼fl oz) maple syrup

1   Grease and preheat a waffle iron.

2   In a large bowl, whisk the egg yolks, oil, buttermilk, baking powder and flour until combined.

3   In a stand mixer with the whisk attachment, whisk the egg whites and salt until stiff peaks form. Add the sugar, a tablespoon at a time, and mix until fully incorporated.

4   Add the egg white mixture to the flour mixture and fold it in using a spatula.

5   Using a ladle or large spoon, transfer one-fifth of the batter at a time to the waffle iron and cook for 3–4 minutes until golden brown. (The first one is usually just a tester, so you will end up with four good ones.)

6   For the filling, whip the cream in a large mixing bowl, using hand-held electric beaters, until slightly thickened. Sift the icing sugar over the mixture and whip until the mixture becomes a thick cream.

7   Combine the prepared fruit in a bowl.

8   Place one waffle in the centre of a serving plate. Add one-quarter of the whipped cream in an even layer over the waffle. Top with one-quarter of the mixed fruit and drizzle with 2 tablespoons of the maple syrup.

9   Repeat until complete, adding some of the extra strawberries with their stems to decorate the top. Slice and serve.

10 This cake is best served as soon as it is assembled, but it can be kept in the fridge for up to 24 hours.

SERVES 6

It wouldn't be brunch without pancakes, so here's my recipe for red-white-and-blue, light, American-style pancakes. Serve them with cream, fresh berries and maple syrup, put on some Miley and Party in the USA!

AMERICAN PANCAKES

1 large egg, room temperature
350ml (12fl oz) buttermilk, room temperature
40g (1½oz) unsalted butter, melted and cooled
40g (1½oz) caster (superfine) sugar
pinch of salt
160g (5½oz) plain (all-purpose) flour
2 teaspoons baking powder
¼ teaspoon each of red and blue gel food colouring
300g (10½oz) double (thick) cream
1 teaspoon vanilla bean paste
4 tablespoons icing (confectioners') sugar, sifted
vegetable oil, for frying
fresh strawberries, sliced, to serve
fresh blueberries, to serve
maple syrup, to drizzle

1   Place the egg, buttermilk and melted butter in a large bowl and whisk until combined.

2   Add the sugar and salt to the wet ingredients, sift the flour and baking powder over the mixture and whisk again until it becomes a thin batter.

3   Divide the batter evenly among three bowls. To one bowl add the red food colouring and to the second bowl add the blue. Mix until well combined and the colours are even. Leave the third bowl plain.

4   Place the cream, vanilla and icing sugar in a stand mixer with the whisk attachment and whip until soft peaks form.

5   Heat a drizzle of oil in a non-stick frying pan over medium heat. Once hot, pour a ladleful of batter into the centre of the pan. Fry for 1–2 minutes on both sides until golden brown, then transfer to a plate lined with paper towel. Repeat with the remaining batter to make six pancakes in each colour, adding more oil as needed.

6   For each serve, place a blue pancake on a plate, then add a plain pancake and finish with a red pancake. Top with the cream, then the strawberries and blueberries. Drizzle with maple syrup and serve.

7   Any leftovers can be stored in the fridge wrapped in plastic wrap for up to 2 days.

Get the party started with these silver-coated chocolate disco balls filled with rich espresso mousse – they are sure to have your guests dancing well into the night.

DISCO BALL ESPRESSO PUDDINGS

CHOCOLATE CASE
160g (5½oz) dark chocolate (70% cocoa solids), chopped
8 silicone hemisphere moulds 7 x 3.5cm (2¾ x 1¼ inches)

ESPRESSO MOUSSE FILLING
1 tablespoon instant espresso powder
1 teaspoon boiling water
100g (3½oz) mascarpone
100g (3½oz) double (thick) cream
30g (1oz) icing (confectioners') sugar, sifted

DECORATION
silver edible spray paint
black edible food marker pen

1   For the chocolate cases, heat half the chocolate in the microwave on High in 20-second bursts, stirring after each burst. Let it sit for 1 minute, then stir the chocolate until it is completely melted.

2   Using a pastry brush, cover the silicone moulds with the chocolate, then set aside to cool in the fridge.

3   Once set, peel the chocolate hemispheres out of the moulds. Repeat steps 1 and 2 to make eight more chocolate hemispheres reserving a little of the melted chocolate to use later.

4   For the filling, combine the coffee and boiling water in a large bowl and stir until the coffee dissolves. Add the mascarpone and mix it using hand-held electric beaters until it becomes light and fluffy.

5   Add the cream and sugar and whisk on high speed until thickened – be careful not to overwhip or it may become grainy.

6   Transfer the mousse to a piping bag with a large plain nozzle and pipe the mixture into the hemispheres until almost full. Use a cake scraper or palette knife to level the surface and remove any excess chocolate.

7   You're now going to use that little bit of left-over melted chocolate you put aside as glue to stick the hemispheres together. (You may need to remelt it if it has set.) Place the melted chocolate in a disposable piping bag with the tip cut off and pipe a rim of chocolate around a hemisphere. Place another hemisphere on top and hold it in place, rims together, for a few seconds until the chocolate has set, then place on the wire rack. Repeat to make eight spheres.

8   Place a length of baking paper under a wire rack and place the spheres on top. Spray the spheres with the edible silver spray – it may take a couple of applications to fully coat them.

9   When the silver spray has dried, use the edible black marker to draw stripes horizontally and vertically around the balls to create a disco-ball look. Store in an airtight container in the fridge for up to 3 days.

SERVES 4

Topped with fluffy cream, fresh fruit and maple syrup, this brunch classic has a colourful twist. You can use my recipe for Rainbow Milk Loaf (page 27) for this French toast, but any milk loaf will do.

RAINBOW CLOUD FRENCH TOAST

150ml (5fl oz) full-cream (whole) milk
2 large eggs, room temperature
1 tablespoon soft light brown sugar
zest of 1 orange
4 thick slices of Rainbow Milk Loaf (page 27) or any milk loaf
200g (7oz) double (thick) cream
2 tablespoons icing (confectioners') sugar, sifted
50g (1¾oz) unsalted butter
50ml (1½fl oz) orange juice
50g (1¾oz) caster (superfine) sugar mixed with ½ teaspoon ground cinnamon
10 fresh raspberries
20 fresh blueberries
10 fresh strawberries, sliced
10 fresh blackberries
maple syrup, to drizzle

1 Combine the milk, eggs, soft light brown sugar and orange zest in a baking tin and whisk with a fork until combined.

2 Add the slices of bread to the tin, turning until they are evenly soaked all over.

3 In a stand mixer with the whisk attachment, whip the cream and icing sugar until soft peaks form. Refrigerate until ready to use.

4 Heat the butter in a large frying pan over medium heat for about 3 minutes.

5 Working in batches, fry the soaked bread on each side for 4 minutes until crisp.

6 Once fried, brush the toast with orange juice and coat with the sugar and cinnamon mixture.

7 Place the French toast on serving plates, top with the whipped cream and fresh fruit and drizzle with maple syrup. Serve immediately.

SERVES 6

What better way to finish brunch than serving this rustic Italian pizza topped with hazelnut chocolate spread, fresh fruit and flaked coconut. This recipe is not only delicious, it also settles one of the biggest debates in history ... pineapple DOES belong on pizza!

FRUIT & CHOCOLATE PIZZA PUDDING

PIZZA BASE

150g (5½oz) strong flour, sifted
1 teaspoon caster (superfine) sugar
¼ teaspoon salt
3g (⅛oz) active dried yeast
110ml (3½fl oz) full-cream (whole) milk
2 teaspoons vegetable oil

TOPPING

100g (3½oz) chocolate hazelnut spread
5 fresh strawberries, halved with leaves still on
1 slice of pineapple
1 kiwi fruit, halved lengthways and sliced
10 fresh raspberries
1 handful fresh blueberries
10g (⅓oz) toasted coconut flakes
10g (⅓oz) dried pineapple flakes

1 For the pizza base, in a stand mixer with the dough hook attachment, mix the flour, sugar, salt, yeast and milk on medium speed for 7 minutes. Add 1 teaspoon of the oil and mix for a further 3 minutes.

2 Cover the bowl with plastic wrap and leave the dough to prove in a warm place for 90 minutes.

3 Preheat the oven to 200°C (400°F). Grease a baking tray and line it with baking paper.

4 Grease your hands and work surface and roll out the dough into a 25cm (10 inch) circle, about 1cm (½ inch) thick, but with the dough slightly higher around the edge to keep the filling in place.

5 Spread the remaining teaspoon of oil in the middle of the pizza. Leave the dough to rest for 15 minutes.

6 Bake for 15 minutes until it is nicely browned at the edge and cooked through.

7 For the topping, melt the hazelnut spread in the microwave on High for 30 seconds.

8 Cover the pizza base with the chocolate hazelnut spread, leaving a 2.5cm (1 inch) border around the edge.

9 Arrange the fresh fruit on top of the pizza. Sprinkle with the coconut and pineapple flakes and serve immediately while still warm – but, like any good pizza, it also tastes great cold.

MAKES 12

With swirls of buttery, sugary cinnamon enveloped in soft bread, these cinnamon buns are topped with a luscious cream cheese frosting and scattered with colourful rainbow sprinkles. They are the perfect sweet treat to serve after a savoury brunch.

CINNAMON FUNFETTI BUNS

CINNAMON BUNS
550g (1lb 4oz) strong flour, sifted
275ml (9¾fl oz) full-cream (whole) milk
10g (⅓oz) active dried yeast
100g (3½oz) caster (superfine) sugar
½ teaspoon salt
2 large eggs, room temperature
80g (2¾oz) unsalted butter, melted and cooled
2 tablespoons rainbow sprinkles, plus extra for sprinkling

FILLING
100g (3½oz) unsalted butter, room temperature
200g (7oz) soft dark brown sugar
4 tablespoons ground cinnamon

CREAM CHEESE FROSTING
50g (1¾oz) unsalted butter, room temperature
125ml (4fl oz) icing (confectioners') sugar, sifted
100g (3½oz) cream cheese, room temperature
2 tablespoons full-cream (whole) milk

1   For the cinnamon buns, in a stand mixer with the dough hook attachment, mix the flour, milk, yeast, sugar, salt and eggs on medium speed for 7 minutes. Add the butter and mix for a further 5 minutes until a smooth dough forms.

2   Cover the bowl with plastic wrap and leave to prove in a warm place for 90 minutes.

3   For the filling, use a stand mixer with the paddle attachment to beat the butter until pale and creamy. Add the sugar and mix until the mixture is pale and creamy and the sugar is fully incorporated. Add the cinnamon and mix briefly to combine.

4   Place the dough on a floured work surface, add the rainbow sprinkles and reknead the dough briefly to distribute the sprinkles throughout.

5   Roll out the dough into a 40 x 30cm (16 x 12 inch) rectangle.

6   Spread the filling over the dough, then roll the dough into a sausage lengthways. Cut the sausage of dough into 12 equal pieces.

7   Line a 35 x 24 x 5cm (14 x 9½ x 2 inch) baking tin with paper and place the buns in it, cut sides down. Cover with a clean tea towel (dish towel) and leave to prove in a warm place for 30 minutes until doubled in size.

8   Preheat the oven to 180°C (350°F).

9   Bake the buns for 20 minutes until a deep golden brown. Leave them to cool in the tin.

10 When the buns are just warm, prepare the frosting.

11 In a stand mixer with the paddle attachment, beat the butter until pale and creamy. Add the sugar and mix until fully incorporated. Add the cream cheese and mix to combine. Finally, mix in the milk until combined and the frosting is smooth.

12 Spread the frosting on top of the buns and scatter some sprinkles on top. Remove from the tin and serve.

13 Store in an airtight container for up to 2 days.

Get ready to taste the rainbow! This chocolate tart is filled with rich chocolate cream, then topped with colourful fresh fruits arranged in a rainbow pattern. It makes a joyous addition to any brunch.

CHOCOLATE & RAINBOW FRUIT TART

CHOCOLATE PASTRY

100g (3½oz) unsalted butter, cold, cubed
175g (6oz) plain (all-purpose) flour, sifted
70g (2½oz) icing (confectioners') sugar, sifted
25g (1oz) pure unsweetened cocoa powder, sifted
2 egg yolks, room temperature

1. In a stand mixer with the paddle attachment, mix the butter, flour, sugar and cocoa powder on low speed until the texture resembles breadcrumbs. Add the egg yolks and mix until a smooth dough forms.

2. Wrap the dough in plastic wrap and refrigerate for 1 hour.

3. Remove the dough from the fridge and let it rest for 10 minutes.

4. On a floured work surface, roll out the dough to fit a 36 x 12cm (14¼ x 4½ inch) baking tin.

5. Grease the tin and line it with the dough.

6. Freeze for 30 minutes.

7. Preheat the oven to 180°C (350°F).

8. Remove the pastry from the freezer. Cover the pastry with baking paper, fill with baking beans and bake for 15 minutes.

9. Remove the beans and paper and bake for a further 15 minutes until the pastry is crisp. Leave to cool in the tin.

CHOCOLATE CREAM

3 egg yolks, room temperature
90g (3¼oz) caster (superfine) sugar
15g (½oz) plain (all-purpose) flour, sifted
15g (½oz) cornflour (cornstarch), sifted
200ml (7fl oz) full-cream (whole) milk
100g (3½oz) double (thick) cream
1 teaspoon vanilla bean paste
80g (2¾oz) dark chocolate (50% cocoa solids), chopped

1. In a stand mixer with the whisk attachment, whisk the egg yolks, sugar and flours until combined.

2. Combine the milk, cream and vanilla bean paste in a medium saucepan over medium heat and bring to the boil.

3. While whisking constantly, add the hot mixture to the stand mixer and whisk to combine.

4. Pour all the mixture back into the saucepan over medium heat and stir constantly until the mixture boils and thickens.

5. Remove from the heat and add the chocolate. Leave for about 30 seconds, then stir the chocolate until melted.

6. Pour the chocolate mixture into the baked tart shell and level the surface. Chill in the fridge for 1 hour.

TO ASSEMBLE

80g (2¾oz) fresh strawberries, quartered
80g (2¾oz) orange segments (no skin or pith)
100g (3½oz) sliced tinned pineapple, cut into chunks
80g (2¾oz) kiwi fruit, sliced
40g (1½oz) fresh blueberries
60g (2¼oz) red grapes

1. Once the tart is cool and the chocolate is set, remove it from the tin.

2. Arrange the fruit on the tart in rainbow colour order (see photograph).

3. Store in the fridge for up to 2 days.

MAKES 12

Racuchy are traditional Polish small apple pancakes. For this version I've paired banana with caramel and whipped cream, which I think is the perfect brunch recipe for you and your guests to enjoy.

BANANA BRUNCH FRITTERS

200g (7oz) plain (all-purpose) flour, sifted
150ml (5fl oz) full-cream (whole) milk
5g (⅛oz) active dried yeast
1 tablespoon caster (superfine) sugar
2 egg yolks, room temperature
1 large banana, sliced
vegetable oil, for frying
hot water
200g (7oz) double (thick) cream
20g (¾oz) icing (confectioners') sugar, sifted
100g (3½oz) caramel (I use store-bought 'caramel drizzle')

1. In a stand mixer with the dough hook attachment, mix the flour, milk, yeast, caster sugar and egg yolks on medium speed for 10 minutes until a sticky dough forms.

2. Fold the banana slices into the dough using a spatula.

3. Cover the bowl and leave the dough to prove in a warm place for about 75 minutes until doubled in size.

4. Heat 1cm (½ inch) of oil in a frying pan over medium heat.

5. Soak a large metal serving spoon in a bowl of hot water.

6. Using the heated spoon, transfer spoonfuls of the dough into the hot oil and fry each side of the fritters for 2 minutes until fluffy and golden brown. Transfer the cooked fritters to a plate lined with paper towel. Repeat with the remaining dough, reheating the spoon in the water before each fritter.

7. Using hand-held electric beaters, whip the cream with the icing sugar until stiff peaks form.

8. Drizzle the fried dough with caramel, top with whipped cream and serve.

9. The fritters are the best eaten within a couple of hours. Serve them hot (or cold if you prefer).

MAKES 6

Candied bacon and maple syrup brunch muffins are the perfect blend of sweet and salty. The light, maple-flavoured muffins contain pieces of salty, candied bacon and will definitely get your brunch guests talking.

BACON & MAPLE SYRUP MUFFINS

4 streaky bacon rashers
160g (5½oz) plain (all-purpose) flour
1 teaspoon baking powder
pinch of salt
75g (2½oz) caster (superfine) sugar
110g (3¾oz) unsalted butter, melted and cooled
1 egg
125ml (4fl oz) buttermilk
60ml (2fl oz) maple syrup
brown sugar, to sprinkle

1   Preheat the oven to 190°C (375°F). Grease a baking tray and line it with baking paper. Line six holes of a muffin tin with paper cases.

2   Place the bacon on the baking tray and bake in the oven for 15 minutes until crisp and a deep golden brown. Remove from the oven and set aside to cool.

3   Chop the bacon into small pieces and place in a small bowl.

4   Sift the flour and baking powder into a bowl, add the salt and sugar and stir to combine.

5   Place the melted butter, egg, buttermilk and maple syrup in a separate large bowl and whisk to combine.

6   Add the dry mixture to the wet mixture and whisk using hand-held electric beaters until combined. Add the bacon and fold it in using a spatula.

7   Pour the batter into the paper cases in the muffin tin until three-quarters full.

8   Add a sprinkling of brown sugar on top of each muffin, then bake for 15 minutes until golden brown on top and a toothpick inserted into the muffins comes out clean.

9   Remove the muffins from the oven and set aside to cool in the tin for a few minutes before placing the warm muffins on a serving tray.

10 Store in an airtight container for up to 2 days.

PRIDE
PARTY

SERVES 8

My rainbow pavlova consists of chic, pastel-coloured, peppermint-flavoured meringue, topped with whipped cream, tart mango curd and fresh fruit. It's the perfect Pride party dessert, leaving guests with breath as fresh as their dance moves, ready for those unexpected encounters.

RAINBOW PAVLOVA

PEPPERMINT MERINGUE

6 large egg whites, room temperature
pinch of salt
300g (10½oz) caster (superfine) sugar
½ teaspoon peppermint essence
1 tablespoon vanilla bean paste
10g (⅓oz) cornflour (cornstarch)
1 teaspoon white vinegar
red, orange, yellow, green, blue and purple gel food colouring

1   Preheat the oven to 140°C (275°F).

2   In a stand mixer with the whisk attachment, whisk the egg whites until slightly frothy. Add the salt and whisk until stiff peaks form. While whisking, gradually add the sugar, a tablespoon at a time, until fully incorporated and the mixture is no longer grainy. Add the peppermint essence and vanilla bean paste and mix well to combine.

3   Sift the cornflour over the mixture and fold it in gently using a spatula. Add the vinegar and fold it in gently.

4   Divide the mixture evenly among six bowls. Add two drops of a different food colouring to each portion and mix until well combined and the colours are even.

5   Draw a 20cm (8 inch) circle on a piece of baking paper, dark enough so you can see it when you turn the paper over.

6   Place the paper, upside down, on a baking tray and dollop all the different-coloured meringue mixtures within the circle outline to form one dome (see photograph).

7   Using a cake scraper or palette knife, smooth the side of the meringue, from bottom to top, to achieve a pavlova look.

8   Put the meringue in the oven and immediately reduce the temperature to 120°C (235°F). Bake for 2 hours and 25 minutes, then leave in the oven for a minimum of 2 hours to cool. Transfer the meringue to a serving plate.

MANGO CURD

2 egg yolks, room temperature
90ml (3fl oz) mango pulp
1 tablespoon lemon juice
40g (1½oz) caster (superfine) sugar
30g (1oz) unsalted butter
1 tablespoon lemon juice

1   Place all the ingredients in a saucepan over high heat and bring to the boil, stirring constantly.

2   Remove the pan from the heat and leave to cool to room temperature.

WHIPPED CREAM

300g (10½oz) double (thick) cream
30g (1oz) icing (confectioners') sugar, sifted
1 teaspoon vanilla bean paste

1   Using hand-held electric beaters, whip the cream with the sugar and vanilla until stiff peaks form.

TO ASSEMBLE

50g (1¾oz) fresh blackberries
50g (1¾oz) fresh raspberries
2 kiwi fruit, sliced
50g (1¾oz) fresh blueberries
50g (1¾oz) pomegranate seeds
6 large fresh strawberries, halved

1   Spoon the whipped cream onto the top of the meringue.

2   Spoon half the curd into the centre of the pavlova, on top of the cream.

3   Top with the fresh fruit and the remaining curd.

4   Serve immediately. You can prepare the meringue for the pavlova a day in advance and store it in a sealed airtight container. Assemble the pavlova just before you're ready to serve it. For a longer-lasting pavlova, consider brushing the top with melted white chocolate. This helps to prevent the pavlova from melting after contact with the cream.

SERVES 12

This colourful vanilla funfetti piñata cake is not only cute, it contains secret candy surprises for your party guests, which are revealed when the first slice is cut! Who will the lucky person be? YOU get to decide!

LLAMA PIÑATA CAKE

SPONGE
200g (7oz) unsalted butter, room temperature
250g (9oz) caster (superfine) sugar
50ml (1½fl oz) vegetable oil
1 tablespoon vanilla bean paste
6 large egg whites, room temperature
250g (9oz) plain (all-purpose) flour
2 teaspoons baking powder
125ml (4fl oz) buttermilk
80g (2¾oz) rainbow sprinkles

1 Preheat the oven to 180°C (350°F). Grease four 15cm (6 inch) round cake tins and line the bases with baking paper.

2 In a stand mixer with the paddle attachment, beat the butter until pale and creamy. While mixing, gradually add the sugar, a tablespoon at a time, until fully incorporated. Add the oil and vanilla and mix until combined. Add the egg whites, one at a time, mixing well after each addition.

3 In another bowl, mix together the flour and baking powder.

4 Sift one-third of the flour mixture over the wet ingredients and fold it in using a spatula.

5 Add one-third of the buttermilk and mix until combined using a spatula.

6 Repeat steps 4 and 5 twice more, until the flour mixture and buttermilk are all used.

7 Add the sprinkles and mix to combine evenly.

8 Divide the batter equally between tins, level the surfaces, then bake for 20 minutes until a toothpick inserted into the cakes comes out clean.

9 Leave the cakes in the tins until cool to the touch, then transfer to a wire rack to cool completely.

PLAIN BUTTERCREAM FILLING
60ml (2fl oz) water
125g (4½oz) caster (superfine) sugar
1 teaspoon vanilla bean paste
6 large egg yolks, room temperature
275g (9¾oz) unsalted butter, room temperature, cubed

1 Place the water and sugar in a small saucepan over high heat and cook until the temperature reaches 117°C (243°F) on a sugar thermometer.

2 In a stand mixer with the whisk attachment, whisk the vanilla bean paste and egg yolks on high speed until light and fluffy. While whisking, slowly add the hot sugar syrup to the eggs. Whisk until the egg mixture reaches room temperature, around 10 minutes.

3 Gradually add the butter, a cube at a time, and whisk until well combined and fluffy.

DECORATIVE BUTTERCREAM

300g (10½oz) unsalted butter, room temperature
300g (10½oz) condensed milk
1 tablespoon vanilla bean paste
⅛ teaspoon each of purple, jade, yellow and pink gel food colouring

1 In a stand mixer with the paddle attachment, beat the butter until pale and creamy. While mixing, add the condensed milk and vanilla bean paste and mix to combine.

2 Divide the buttercream evenly among four bowls. Add a different food colouring to each portion and mix until well combined and the colours are even.

3 Transfer the buttercream to piping bags with grass-effect nozzles.

TO ASSEMBLE

surprise candy such as jelly hearts, jelly rings, jelly eggs, candy watches, candy necklaces – the choice is yours
60g (2oz) black fondant icing
15g (½oz) pink fondant icing

1 Using a 5cm (2 inch) cookie cutter, cut a circle out of the centre of three of the sponges. (Put the offcuts aside, as you will use one of the circle cut-outs to make the ears.)

2 Place one of the hollowed sponges in the centre of a cake board or serving plate, then cover the rim with plain buttercream filling.

3 Top with the second hollowed sponge and again cover the rim with buttercream.

4 Repeat with the third hollowed sponge and cover the rim with buttercream.

5 Fill the centre of the cake to the brim with the surprise candy.

6 Top the cake with the fourth sponge and cover the entire cake with the plain buttercream.

7 Make two ears for the llama by cutting one of the cut-out circles in half. Secure the ears in place on top of the cake using buttercream.

8 Cover the cake with the decorative buttercreams, starting from the bottom, alternating colours to achieve a striped rainbow effect (see photograph). Cover the ears with one colour and use a different colour for the insides of the ears.

9 Once the cake is fully covered, roll out the fondant icings by hand and make your llama's cute eyes, nose and mouth.

10 Store at room temperature for up to 2 days.

MAKES 12

These plain gingerbread people are in desperate need of a drag makeover. Let your party guests decorate these spicy queens with an assortment of sweets, fondant icing and decorations and watch the creativity flow!

GINGERBREAD QUEENS

GINGERBREAD COOKIES

90g (3¼oz) unsalted butter, room temperature
90g (3¼oz) soft dark brown sugar
1 large egg yolk, room temperature
50g (1¾oz) runny honey
200g (7oz) plain (all-purpose) flour
1½ tablespoons ground cinnamon
1½ teaspoons ground ginger
¼ teaspoon ground cloves
¼ teaspoon allspice
¼ teaspoon ground nutmeg
½ teaspoon bicarbonate of soda (baking soda)
pinch of salt

DECORATION

assorted candy
coloured fondant icing of your choice
edible cake decorations, such as eyes, icing pens, cola bottles, jellies, jelly laces, pearls
caramel or edible glue, for attaching the decorations

1   Grease a baking tray and line it with baking paper.

2   In a stand mixer with the paddle attachment, beat the butter and sugar until pale and creamy. Add the egg yolk and honey and mix until combined.

3   Sift the remaining ingredients over the mixture and mix until a soft dough forms.

4   Wrap the dough in plastic wrap and refrigerate for 60 minutes.

5   Remove the dough from the fridge. On a generously floured work surface, roll out the dough until 3mm (1⁄16 inch) thick.

6   Using a 10cm (4 inch) gingerbread person cookie cutter, cut out 12 shapes and place them on the baking tray.

7   Place the tray in the freezer for 15 minutes.

8   Preheat the oven to 180°C (350°F).

9   Remove the tray from the freezer and bake for 10 minutes until the edges are firm when gently touched. Cool for a few minutes on the tray, then transfer to a wire rack to cool completely.

10 Lay out an assortment of candy, coloured fondant icing and edible cake decorations in individual bowls and serve to your guests along with their gingerbread queens. You can either use caramel or edible glue for attaching the decorations.

11 Store in an airtight container for up to 2 weeks.

SERVES 8

Fun and fresh, this watermelon-themed cake consists of a layer of spinach and lemon sponge with a sweet cream filling topped with strawberry jelly and blueberries. It's a delicious way to eat your greens!

WATERMELON JELLY LAYER CAKE

200g (7oz) baby spinach
zest of 2 lemons, plus the juice of
    1 lemon
2 large eggs, room temperature
100g (3½oz) caster (superfine)
    sugar
100ml (3½fl oz) vegetable oil
160g (5½oz) plain (all-purpose)
    flour
1½ teaspoons baking powder
1 teaspoon bicarbonate of soda
    (baking soda)
125g (4½oz) mascarpone
30g (1oz) icing (confectioners')
    sugar, sifted
125g (4½oz) double (thick) cream
50g (1¾oz) white chocolate,
    grated
50g (1¾oz) fresh blueberries
1 packet strawberry jelly (gelatine
    dessert) powder (enough to set
    600ml/21fl oz water)
350ml (12fl oz) boiling water

1 Preheat the oven to 160°C (315°F). Line a 20cm (8 inch) round springform cake tin with baking paper and grease generously.

2 Add the spinach, half the lemon zest and 1 teaspoon of the lemon juice to a blender and blitz until smooth.

3 In a stand mixer with the whisk attachment, whisk the eggs and caster sugar until light and fluffy. While whisking, gradually add the oil and mix to combine.

4 Add the blended spinach mixture and fold it in using a spatula until fully combined.

5 Sift the flour, baking powder and bicarbonate of soda over the mixture and fold them in until the mixture is smooth.

6 Pour the batter into the tin, level the surface, then bake for 30 minutes until a toothpick inserted into the cake comes out clean. Leave to cool in the tin.

7 Remove from the tin and, using a cake wire or serrated knife, level the top of the cake, then return the cake to the tin.

8 In a stand mixer with the whisk attachment, whip the mascarpone, icing sugar and cream until thickened. Add the grated white chocolate and remaining lemon zest and juice and fold them in using a spatula.

9 Spread the mixture over the sponge and level the top.

10 Evenly distribute the blueberries over the cream and press them in to resemble watermelon seeds.

11 Dissolve the jelly powder in the boiling water and set aside to cool.

12 Once the jelly is starting to set, pour it on top of the cake in the tin.

13 Refrigerate the cake until the jelly has fully set.

14 Remove the cake from the tin (use a kitchen blowtorch to warm the sides of the tin to make it easier). Place on a cake plate and serve.

15 Store in the fridge for up to 3 days.

SERVES 10

This moist citrus sponge is soaked in a heady bath of vodka, drizzled with a lemon–lime soda icing and topped with lemon peel. It's sure to get your guests in the party mood!

VODKA & LEMONADE CAKE

VODKA & LEMONADE CAKE
125g (4½oz) unsalted butter, room temperature
180g (6¼oz) caster (superfine) sugar
1 teaspoon vanilla bean paste
1 teaspoon lemon zest
1 teaspoon lime zest
1 teaspoon lemon juice
2 large eggs, room temperature
170g (5¾oz) plain (all-purpose) flour
1 teaspoon baking powder
90ml (3fl oz) lemon–lime soda (e.g. Sprite)
20ml (½fl oz) vodka

VODKA & LEMONADE SOAK
60ml (2fl oz) lemon-lime soda (e.g., Sprite)
30ml (1fl oz) vodka

LEMON–LIME & SODA ICING
125g (4½oz) icing (confectioners') sugar, sifted
1 tablespoon lemon juice
2 tablespoons lemon–lime soda (e.g., Sprite)

LEMON DECORATION
2 organic unwaxed lemons

1   Preheat the oven to 180°C (350°F). Generously grease an 18.5 x 11 x 8.5cm (7¼ x 4¼ x 3¼ inch) loaf (bar) tin.

2   For the cake, in a stand mixer with the paddle attachment, beat the butter until pale and creamy. While mixing, gradually add the sugar, a tablespoon at a time, until fully incorporated. Add the vanilla bean paste, the zests and lemon juice and mix until light and fluffy. While mixing, add the eggs one at a time, mixing well after each addition, until the mixture is smooth.

3   Sift one-third of the flour and one-third of the baking powder over the batter mixture and fold them in using a spatula.

4   Mix the lemon–lime soda and vodka together in a small bowl or cup, then add one-third to the batter and fold it in using a spatula.

5   Repeat steps 3 and 4 until the dry ingredients and the liquid are all used.

6   Transfer the batter to the tin, level the surface, then bake for 45 minutes until a toothpick inserted into the cake comes out clean. Leave to cool in the tin.

7   For the soak, mix the vodka and lemon–lime soda together in a small bowl or cup.

8   Invert the cool cake onto a serving plate. Poke holes in the cake with a skewer and drizzle the soak over the top.

9   For the icing, mix all the ingredients together in a bowl, then drizzle the icing over the top of the cake, allowing some to drip down the side.

10   To make the lemon decoration, use a canelle knife to cut thin strips from the lemon peel. Or use a sharp knife to peel the lemon, removing any white pith, then cut the peel into very thin strips. Use the lemon to decorate the top of the cake (see photograph).

11   Store in an airtight container for up to 2 days.

SERVES 10

This cute bear cake represents my body type, as it is known within my community. Soft and squidgy, the cake is made up of chocolate sponge, spiced buttercream and plum butter and is decorated with fondant icing.

BEAR CAKE

CHOCOLATE SPONGE

300g (10½oz) caster (superfine) sugar
150g (5½oz) soft dark brown sugar
375ml (13fl oz) buttermilk
190ml (6½fl oz) vegetable oil
2 tablespoons natural vanilla extract
2 tablespoons soy sauce
3 large eggs, room temperature
150g (5½oz) pure unsweetened cocoa powder
375g (13oz) plain (all-purpose) flour
3 teaspoons bicarbonate of soda (baking soda)
2 teaspoons baking powder
375ml (13fl oz) freshly brewed, very strong coffee

1   Preheat the oven to 175°C (345°F). Generously grease three 15cm (6 inch) round springform cake tins.

2   In a large bowl using hand-held electric beaters, whisk the sugars, buttermilk, oil, vanilla, soy sauce and eggs.

3   Combine the cocoa, flour, bicarbonate of soda and baking powder in a separate bowl.

4   Sift the dry ingredients gradually over the wet mixture, in three batches, mixing to combine. Add the hot coffee and mix until combined.

5   Distribute the batter evenly between the tins, level the tops, then bake for 45 minutes until a toothpick inserted into the cakes comes out with just a few crumbs but no raw batter. Leave to cool in the tins, then remove the cakes from the tins and place on a wire rack.

SPICED BUTTERCREAM

300g (10½oz) unsalted butter, room temperature
75g (2½oz) treacle
300g (10½oz) icing (confectioners') sugar, sifted
1 large orange
1 tablespoon natural vanilla extract
1½ tablespoons ground cinnamon
1 teaspoon ground ginger
⅛ teaspoon ground cloves
⅛ teaspoon ground nutmeg
⅛ teaspoon ground cardamom

1   In a stand mixer with the paddle attachment, beat the butter until pale and creamy. Add the treacle and mix to combine. While mixing, add the sugar gradually, a tablespoon at a time, until fully incorporated.

2   Zest the orange, cut it in half and juice one half.

3   Combine the zest and orange juice in a bowl with the vanilla and spices, then add this mixture to the buttercream and mix until stiff.

4   Transfer the buttercream to a piping bag with a large plain nozzle.

TO ASSEMBLE

200g (7oz) plum butter
600g (1lb 5oz) brown fondant icing
cornflour (cornstarch), to dust
50g (1¾oz) light beige fondant
  icing
50g (1¾oz) black fondant icing
10g (⅓oz) white fondant icing

1   Carve one of the sponges into a
    dome shape and set aside.

2   Place one of the remaining whole
    sponges on a cake board or serving
    plate and cover it with one-quarter of
    the spiced buttercream.

3   Pipe a border of buttercream around
    the edge of the cake to act as a dam
    to stop the plum butter from leaking
    out when you add it.

4   Fill the centre with half of the plum
    butter.

5   Place the other whole sponge on top
    and repeat with the buttercream and
    remaining plum butter.

6   Top with the domed sponge.
    Pipe zig-zag lines of buttercream
    all over the cake. Using a cake
    scraper or palette knife, gently
    spread the buttercream across the
    cake, ensuring it covers the cake
    completely. For a very smooth
    surface, position your scraper so it's
    barely touching the edge of the cake,
    then gently glide it all the way around
    the cake.

7   Knead the brown fondant icing
    and roll it out until 5mm (¼ inch) thick,
    dusting it with cornflour to prevent it
    from sticking – you will need the
    sheet of icing to be large enough to
    cover the top and side of the cake.

8   Cover the cake with the sheet of
    brown fondant icing, starting from
    the top and working your way down
    the side gently, to avoid creases.

    Trim the excess fondant icing at
    the bottom of the cake.

9   Roll the trimmed-off fondant icing
    into a ball. Shape the ball into a round
    dimpled disc, then cut in half. Use
    a little bit of water to attach the two
    halves to the top of the cake dome
    to resemble ears.

10 Knead and roll the beige fondant
    icing out into a circle about 7.5cm
    (3 inches) in diameter.

11 Roll a small walnut-sized ball of the
    black fondant icing and place it in
    the middle of the beige circle to
    represent a nose, using a little water
    to secure it in place.

12 Using a pointed icing modelling tool,
    or a toothpick, draw an indented line,
    starting from the nose, to make a
    smiley face, then stick the bear's face
    onto the centre of the cake using a
    little water to secure it.

13 Knead and roll out the remaining
    black fondant icing into two circles,
    each about 2.5cm (1 inch) in diameter.

14 Knead and roll out the white fondant
    icing into two smaller circles, each
    about 5mm (¼ inch) in diameter.

15 Stick the white circles onto the black
    circles to create the bear's eyes. Use
    a little bit of water to stick the eyes
    onto the face.

16 Store at room temperature for up to
    2 days.

If your friends like piña colada and getting caught in the rain, give them an umbrella and serve them this delicious cake – coconut rum-soaked sponge with layers of cream and pineapple filling, decorated to look like a pineapple.

PIÑA COLADA CAKE

VANILLA SPONGE

4 large eggs, room temperature, separated
130g (4½oz) caster (superfine) sugar
1 tablespoon natural vanilla extract
100g (3½oz) plain (all-purpose) flour
40g (1½oz) cornflour (cornstarch)

1   Preheat the oven to 180°C (350°F). Line the base of two 15cm (6 inch) round springform cake tins with baking paper.

2   In a stand mixer with the whisk attachment, whisk the egg whites until stiff peaks form. While whisking, gradually add the sugar, a tablespoon at a time, until fully incorporated and the mixture is no longer grainy.

3   In a small bowl, whisk the egg yolks with the vanilla.

4   Pour the egg yolk mixture into the stand mixer while mixing on low speed, until combined.

5   In a separate bowl, combine the flour and cornflour.

6   Sift the flour mixture over the wet mixture in three batches, folding it in using a spatula after each addition until combined.

7   Evenly distribute the mixture between the baking tins. Level the surfaces, then bake for 25 minutes until the tops of the cakes spring back when pressed with a finger and a toothpick inserted into the cakes comes out clean. Leave to cool completely in the tins.

8   Once cool, run a sharp knife around the sides of the cakes to remove them from the tins.

9   Cut the two sponges in half horizontally to make four thinner sponges.

PINEAPPLE FILLING

1 teaspoon gelatine powder
1½ tablespoons cold water
1 x 400g (14oz) tin of pineapple slices in juice
2 teaspoons cornflour (cornstarch)
juice of ½ lemon

1   In a bowl, mix the gelatine powder with the water and leave to soak for 10 minutes.

2   Strain the pineapple – reserving the juice – and cut the fruit into very small cubes.

3   In a small bowl or cup, mix the cornflour with 1 tablespoon water to create a paste.

4   Combine the pineapple cubes and the pineapple and lemon juices in a small saucepan over medium heat and bring to the boil. Add the cornflour mixture and cook for 1 minute, stirring, until thickened – do not cook for longer than 1 minute.

5   Remove the pan from the heat, add the gelatine mixture and mix to combine.

6   Refrigerate for 4 hours until set.

CREAM FILLING

350g (12oz) mascarpone, chilled
175g (6oz) condensed milk,
  chilled overnight

1 In a stand mixer with the whisk attachment, whisk the mascarpone on high speed until light and fluffy. Add the condensed milk and mix until combined. Refrigerate until ready to use.

DECORATIVE BUTTERCREAM

300g (10½oz) unsalted butter,
  room temperature
280g (10oz) condensed milk
1 tablespoon coconut rum
⅛ teaspoon black gel food
  colouring
3 drops red gel food colouring
½ teaspoon yellow gel
  food colouring

1 In a stand mixer with the paddle attachment, beat the butter until pale and creamy. While mixing, add the condensed milk and coconut rum, mixing until combined.

2 Remove 3 tablespoons of the mixture from the bowl and transfer to a separate bowl. Add the black food colouring and mix until combined and the colour is even.

3 Transfer the black buttercream to a piping bag with a small plain nozzle.

4 Add both the red and yellow food colourings to the remaining buttercream and mix until combined and the colour is even.

5 Transfer the bright yellow buttercream to a large piping bag with a star nozzle.

DECORATION

150g (5½oz) white chocolate,
  chopped
½ teaspoon dark green gel food
  colouring

1 Heat the white chocolate in the microwave on High in 30-second bursts, stirring after each burst, until melted.

2 Add the green food colouring to the melted chocolate and mix until the colour is even.

3 Line a baking tray with baking paper.

4 Using a teaspoon, spread the chocolate onto the baking paper in long streaks to resemble pineapple leaves (see photograph). Set aside to cool and set in the fridge.

TO ASSEMBLE

100ml (3½fl oz) coconut rum

1 Place one of the baked sponges in the centre of a 25cm (10 inch) cake board or serving plate and soak with one-quarter of the coconut rum.

2 Place one-third of the pineapple filling on top of the sponge and spread it over the surface evenly.

3 Add one-third of the cream filling on top of the pineapple filling and spread it over the surface evenly.

4 Repeat this process with the next two sponges, then place the remaining sponge on top and soak with the last of the rum.

5 Pipe the decorative buttercream over the top and side of the cake in individual blobs to achieve a pineapple-like effect (see photograph).

6 Remove your green chocolate leaves from the fridge and gently insert them vertically into the top of the cake.

7 Pipe the black buttercream onto the side of the cake to create eyes and a mouth.

8 Store in the fridge for up to 2 days but serve at room temperature.

What's better to accompany a Pride party playlist than these bubblegum-flavoured cake-pop divas, decorated to represent your favourite queens and princesses of pop.

CAKE-POP DIVAS

BUBBLEGUM CAKE

80g (2¾oz) unsalted butter, room temperature
100g (3½oz) caster (superfine) sugar
1 large egg, room temperature
⅛ teaspoon pink gel food colouring
130g (4½oz) plain (all-purpose) flour
1 teaspoon baking powder
1 teaspoon bubblegum flavouring
30ml (1fl oz) full-cream (whole) milk

1. Preheat the oven to 180°C (350°F). Grease a 15cm (6 inch) round springform cake tin and line it with baking paper.

2. In a stand mixer with the paddle attachment, beat the butter until pale and creamy. While mixing, add the sugar gradually, a tablespoon at a time, until fully incorporated. Add the egg and food colouring and mix to combine.

3. Sift the flour and baking powder over the mixture and fold them in using a spatula.

4. In a cup or bowl, combine the bubblegum flavouring and milk, then add this mixture to the batter and mix well to combine.

5. Transfer the batter to the tin, level the surface, then bake for 20 minutes until a toothpick inserted into the cake comes out clean. Set aside to completely cool in the tin.

BUTTERCREAM

75g (2½oz) unsalted butter, room temperature
½ teaspoon natural vanilla extract
150g (5½oz) icing (confectioners') sugar, sifted

1. In a stand mixer with the paddle attachment, beat the butter until pale and creamy. Add the vanilla and mix to combine. While mixing, gradually add the sugar, a tablespoon at a time, until fully incorporated.

TO ASSEMBLE
200g (7oz) vanilla candy melts
12 popsicle sticks
brown and pink gel food colouring
coloured fondant icing (depending
 on your chosen divas' hair
 colour)
24 edible eyes
set of edible food markers

1 Remove the cake from the tin and crumble into small pieces. Place in a bowl with the buttercream. Mix together using a spatula.

2 Divide the mixture into 12 equal portions and roll each into a ball.

3 Place the balls on a baking tray lined with baking paper.

4 Put five candy melts in a bowl and heat them in the microwave on High for 15 seconds, until melted.

5 Dip the end of each popsicle stick into the melted candy, then insert the candy-covered end of the stick into each cake ball.

6 Refrigerate the cake pops for 1 hour.

7 Heat the remaining candy melts in the microwave on High in 30-second bursts, stirring after each burst, until melted.

8 Depending on what skin tones you want for your celebrity divas, mix the food colourings with the melted candy in separate bowls.

9 Dip each cake pop completely into the melted candy colour of your choice, then set aside in a cake pop stand or stuck upright into a piece of styrofoam, to set.

10 Once set, use the different-coloured fondant icings to create the iconic hairstyles of your chosen divas.

11 Decorate each cake pop face with the edible eyes and hair, and draw on lips and other facial features using the edible food markers and more fondant icing to bring your cake pop divas to life.

12 Store them at a cool room temperature for up to 3 days.

SERVES 8

With layers of sweet shortcrust pastry, raspberry jelly with fresh raspberries, sweet mascarpone and whipped cream, all topped with a slow-baked meringue cloud, this cake is absolutely bursting with delicious flavours and textures.

RASPBERRY SPRINKLE CLOUD CAKE

SHORTCRUST PASTRY

65g (2¼oz) unsalted butter, cold, cubed
30g (1oz) icing (confectioners') sugar, sifted
100g (3½oz) plain (all-purpose) flour, sifted
½ teaspoon baking powder, sifted
2 large egg yolks, room temperature
1 teaspoon vanilla bean paste

1   In a stand mixer with the paddle attachment, mix the butter, sugar, flour and baking powder on low speed until the texture resembles breadcrumbs. Add the egg yolks and vanilla bean paste and mix until a smooth dough forms.

2   Wrap the dough in plastic wrap and refrigerate for 60 minutes.

3   Preheat the oven to 190°C (375°F). Line the base of a 20cm (8 inch) round springform cake tin with baking paper.

4   On a floured work surface, roll out the dough until it fits the base of your tin.

5   Press the dough into the base of the tin.

6   Freeze the dough for 15 minutes.

7   Remove from the freezer and bake for 15 minutes until a light golden brown. Leave to cool in the tin.

RASPBERRY JELLY LAYER

2 packets raspberry jelly (gelatine dessert) powder (enough to set 600ml/21fl oz water)
600ml (21fl oz) almost boiling water
350g (12oz) fresh raspberries

1   Stir the jelly powder into the hot water, then let it cool to room temperature.

2   Add the raspberries and transfer the jelly to the fridge until it begins to set – I check every 5 minutes.

3   Line the sides of the tin that contains the pastry with a 10cm (4 inch) high baking paper or cellophane collar.

4   Once the jelly starts to set, pour it onto the pastry base in the tin.

5   Refrigerate for 1 hour or until the jelly is fully set.

WHIPPED CREAM LAYER

300g (10½oz) double (thick) cream
150g (5½oz) mascarpone
50g (1¾oz) icing (confectioners') sugar, sifted
1 teaspoon vanilla bean paste

1   In a stand mixer with the whisk attachment, whip all the ingredients until soft peaks form.

2   Remove the cake from the fridge and add the cream on top of the set jelly. Return to the fridge.

MERINGUE

2 egg whites, room temperature
110g (3¾oz) caster (superfine)
  sugar
1 teaspoon vanilla bean paste
½ teaspoon white vinegar
½ teaspoon cornflour (cornstarch)
rainbow sprinkles

1 Preheat the oven to 140°C (275°F).

2 In a stand mixer with the whisk attachment, whisk the egg whites until stiff peaks form. While whisking, gradually add the sugar, a tablespoon at a time, until the sugar is fully incorporated and the mixture is no longer grainy. Add the vanilla bean paste and vinegar and mix to combine.

3 Sift the cornflour over the mixture and fold it in using a spatula.

4 Transfer the meringue to a piping bag with a large plain nozzle.

5 Draw a 20cm (8 inch) circle on a piece of baking paper, dark enough so you can see it when you turn the paper over. Place the baking paper upside down on a baking tray.

6 Pipe the meringue inside the outline of the circle, creating a cloud-like effect (see photograph). Scatter with the rainbow sprinkles.

7 Place in the oven and immediately reduce the temperature to 120°C (235°F). Bake for 60 minutes until the meringue is crispy and easily peels off the baking paper. Leave to cool on a wire rack.

TO ASSEMBLE

1 Remove the cake from the tin (use a kitchen blowtorch to warm the sides of the tin to make it easier), and place it on a cake board or serving plate. Carefully peel off the paper or cellophane.

2 Top with the meringue cloud and serve.

3 Store in the fridge for up to 2 days.

JANUSZ SAYS

This cake offers endless possibilities for variations, allowing you to customise the flavours to your liking. Swap the raspberries for strawberries and use strawberry jelly, or experiment with tinned pineapple and pineapple jelly.

MAKES 6

A childhood classic, these iced buns are made from sweet, light bread buns and are topped with sugar icing and rainbow sprinkles. They are sure to get your party guests feeling like big kids again.

NOSTALGIC ICED BUNS

FINGER BUNS
250g (9oz) strong flour, sifted
2 tablespoons powdered milk
130ml (4½fl oz) full-cream (whole) milk
1 large egg yolk, room temperature
2 tablespoons caster (superfine) sugar
pinch of salt
7g (¼oz) active dried yeast
35g (1¼oz) unsalted butter, melted and cooled
2 teaspoons rainbow sprinkles

ICING
3 tablespoons hot water
250g (9oz) icing (confectioners') sugar, sifted
pink gel food colouring

1 For the buns, in a stand mixer with the dough hook attachment, mix the flour, powdered milk, full-cream milk, egg yolk, caster sugar, salt and yeast on medium speed for 5 minutes. Add the melted butter and mix for a further 5 minutes.

2 Cover the bowl with plastic wrap and leave to prove in a warm place for 90 minutes.

3 Grease a baking tray and line it with baking paper.

4 Punch the dough down and knead it briefly on a floured work surface.

5 Divide the dough into six equal portions and shape each portion into a 12cm (4½ inch) log.

6 Place the buns on the tray, leaving small gaps between them. Cover with a clean tea towel (dish towel) and leave to prove in a warm place for 30 minutes.

7 Preheat the oven to 180°C (350°F).

8 Bake for 16 minutes until golden brown. Transfer to a wire rack to cool.

9 Prepare the icing by mixing the hot water, sugar and two drops of pink food colouring in a small bowl.

10 Use a teaspoon to spread the icing in a smooth layer on top of each bun. Add the rainbow sprinkles and serve.

11 These are best on the day of baking, but they can be stored in an airtight container for up to 2 days.

I was born in 1988 so my party life has been heavily influenced by the 80s and 90s. This cake has a cola-flavoured sponge inspired by my favourite childhood flavour, and is decorated with neon-coloured drip, stripes and piping inspired by 80s and 90s club nights that I enjoy as an adult today. The cake is best served to the sounds of 80s and 90s club classics.

80s NEON PARTY CAKE

COLA SPONGE

225g (8oz) soft dark brown sugar
150ml (5fl oz) vegetable oil
1 teaspoon vanilla bean paste
2 large eggs, room temperature
230ml (7¾fl oz) cola
300g (10½oz) plain (all-purpose) flour
70g (2½oz) black cocoa powder (available in baking shops and online)
2 teaspoons baking powder
1 teaspoon bicarbonate of soda (baking soda)

1   Preheat the oven to 180°C (350°F). Grease three deep 15cm (6 inch) round springform cake tins and line the bases with baking paper.

2   In a large bowl, whisk the sugar, oil, vanilla bean paste and eggs until combined. Add the cola and whisk to combine. Sift the dry ingredients over the mixture and whisk until fully combined.

3   Distribute the mixture evenly between the three baking tins, level the surfaces, then bake for 35 minutes until a toothpick inserted into the cakes comes out clean. Leave to cool in the tins.

NEON BUTTERCREAM

400g (14oz) unsalted butter, room temperature
400g (14oz) condensed milk
1 tablespoon vanilla bean paste
25g (1oz) black cocoa powder (available in baking shops and online)
½ teaspoon each of orange and pink neon gel food colouring

1   In a stand mixer with the paddle attachment, beat the butter until pale and creamy. Add the condensed milk and vanilla bean paste and mix until combined.

2   Divide the buttercream evenly between two bowls. Add the black cocoa powder to one portion and mix until well combined and the colour is even.

3   Divide the remaining half evenly between two small bowls. Add a different neon food colouring to each portion and mix until well combined and the colours are even.

NEON DRIP

1¾ tablespoons double (thick) cream
85g (3oz) white chocolate, chopped
¼ teaspoon neon yellow gel food colouring

1   Heat the cream in a small saucepan over medium heat until it is just starting to boil.

2   Remove the pan from the heat and add the white chocolate and the neon yellow food colouring. Wait 2 minutes, then stir until the chocolate is fully melted and the mixture is even in colour.

3   Allow the mixture to cool slightly, then transfer to a drip bottle.

TO ASSEMBLE

selection of your favourite retro candy (bananas, shrimp, cola bottles etc.)

1 Use a cake wire or serrated knife to level the tops of the cakes.

2 Place the first cake on a cake board or serving plate and cover the top with one-third of the orange buttercream.

3 Place the second sponge on top and cover with one-third of the pink buttercream.

4 Add the third sponge on top, upside down, and cover the entire cake stack with the black buttercream. Smooth it using a cake scraper or palette knife.

5 Sitting the cake on a turntable (if you have one), or just turning the plate on your work surface, use a small palette knife or the end of a butter knife to remove two 2cm (¾ inch) strips of black buttercream from the cake – one about one-third up from the base, and the other about two-thirds from the base (see photograph).

6 Fill each of these gaps with a little more of the pink and orange neon buttercreams.

7 Use a cake scraper to smooth the sides of the cake again.

8 Refrigerate the cake for 30 minutes.

9 Using the yellow neon colour, create a drip effect on the cake by running the bottle around the edge of the cake, gently squeezing the bottle (see photograph).

10 Cover the top of the cake with the remaining drip mixture to the edge and smooth.

11 Refrigerate the cake for 15 minutes.

12 Remove the cake from the fridge and, using the remaining pink and orange buttercreams, pipe rosettes around the top edge of the cake in a circular formation.

13 Fill the centre of the piped rosettes with retro candy, serve and party like it's 1999!

14 Store at room temperature for up to 2 days.

JANUSZ SAYS

Have you ever come across incredibly rich, super-dark chocolate desserts in bakeries? Have you wondered why replicating that deep, distinctive flavour at home is such a challenge? The answer is black cocoa. Black cocoa doesn't just go through the typical alkalisation process. It's subjected to an ultra Dutching process, intensifying its colour and flavour but without any acidity.

SERVES 8–10

This croquembouche is made with tropical fruit-filled profiteroles. Constructed with delicious sweet caramel and topped with edible sugar butterflies, this tower makes a perfect party centrepiece and will make your guests feel like they're at Club Tropicana (though you need to tell them that the drinks aren't free).

TROPICAL CROQUEMBOUCHE TOWER

FILLING

450g (1lb) frozen mango chunks
450g (1lb) frozen pineapple chunks
juice of 1 lemon
100g (3½oz) caster (superfine) sugar
50g (1¾oz) double (thick) cream
50ml (1½fl oz) full-cream (whole) milk
6 large egg yolks, room temperature
2 teaspoons vanilla bean paste
20g (¾oz) plain (all-purpose) flour
20g (¾oz) cornflour (cornstarch)
2 platinum gelatine leaves
100ml (3½fl oz) water
300g (10½oz) double (thick) cream
50g (1¾oz) icing (confectioners') sugar, sifted

1. In a large saucepan over medium–high heat, combine the mango, pineapple, lemon juice and 50g (1¾oz) of the caster sugar and cook for around 15 minutes until the fruit is falling apart and the mixture has thickened and reduced.

2. Blend with a hand-held blender, then strain the mixture into a bowl to obtain around 450ml (16fl oz) of purée.

3. Return the purée to the pan, add the cream and milk and bring to the boil. Remove from the heat but keep hot.

4. In a stand mixer with the whisk attachment, whisk the egg yolks with the remaining caster sugar and vanilla bean paste until light and fluffy. Sift the flour and cornflour over the mixture and mix to combine.

5. While whisking on medium–low speed, slowly pour half the hot fruit mixture into the egg mixture and mix until combined. Return all the mixture to the pan and heat, whisking constantly until boiling.

6. Transfer the mixture to a bowl, cover with plastic wrap touching the surface, to prevent a skin forming, and refrigerate until chilled.

7. Soak the gelatine in the water for 10 minutes.

8. Whip the cream using hand-held electric beaters until soft peaks form. Add the icing sugar and mix to combine.

9. Squeeze the excess moisture from the gelatine, then melt it in the microwave on High for 5 seconds.

10. Add the gelatine to the cream and whip for 10 seconds.

11. Fold the cream into the cooled fruit mixture.

12. Transfer the mixture to a piping bag with a plain nozzle. Refrigerate until ready to use.

CHOUX PASTRY

250ml (9fl oz) water
125g (4½oz) unsalted butter
150g (5½oz) plain (all-purpose)
  flour
4 large eggs

1. Preheat the oven to 190°C (375°F). Grease two baking trays and line them with baking paper.

2. Combine the water and butter in a saucepan over medium–high heat and bring to the boil.

3. Add the flour and quickly mix using a spatula to combine. The dough is ready when it's shiny, no longer sticking to the bottom of the pan, and forming a ball. Set the pan aside for the dough to cool a little.

4. In a separate bowl, whisk the eggs.

5. Whisking constantly, gradually add the eggs to the dough and mix to combine.

6. Transfer the mixture to a piping bag with a plain nozzle.

7. Pipe 40–50 x 2.5cm (1 inch) balls onto the baking trays. Leave a little space between them as they will spread.

8. Bake for 20 minutes.

9. Open the oven door and poke two holes in the base of each profiterole with a skewer. Close the door and bake for another 5 minutes, then turn the oven off. Open the oven door and let the profiteroles cool inside with the door open.

10. Once cool, use a knife to poke a hole in the bottom of each just big enough to fit the piping nozzle.

CARAMEL

300g (10½oz) caster (superfine)
  sugar
75ml (2¼fl oz) water

1. Combine the sugar and water in a saucepan over medium–high heat and cook until the mixture is an amber colour.

TO ASSEMBLE

15 edible butterfly cupcake
  toppers

1. Pipe cream into each baked profiterole through the hole created with the knife, until the profiterole feels full and heavy.

2. Using tongs, dip the top of each profiterole in the caramel and let the excess drip off, then set aside to let the caramel set.

3. Once the profiteroles are set, build your tower. For the first row, make a circle of nine profiteroles. Dip the side of each profiterole in the caramel and place it on a cake board or stand around 20cm (8 inches) in diameter, with the caramel side facing out.

4. For the next row, dip the side of a profiterole in caramel and place it in the middle of two profiteroles on the bottom row.

5. Build the tower to the top, finishing with two profiteroles glued together and a single one on top (see photograph).

6. Decorate with edible butterflies.

7. The cake is best eaten within 5 hours.

Get ready for a dessert that will take you back to your childhood! This jaffa cake is everything you love about the classic treat, but super-sized and even more delicious. Layers of sponge, orange jelly and chocolate mousse deliver a nostalgic hit. To find out how to segment an orange, I suggest watching a YouTube video.

XXL JAFFA CAKE

SPONGE
1 large egg, room temperature, separated
40g (1½oz) caster (superfine) sugar
25g (1oz) plain (all-purpose) flour
10g (⅓oz) cornflour (cornstarch)

1 Preheat the oven to 180°C (350°F). Line the base of a 15cm (6 inch) round springform cake tin with baking paper.

2 In a stand mixer with the whisk attachment, whisk the egg white until stiff peaks form. While whisking, gradually add the sugar, a teaspoon at a time, until fully incorporated and the mixture is no longer grainy. Add the egg yolk and mix to combine.

3 Sift the flour and cornflour over the mixture and fold them in using a spatula.

4 Transfer the batter to the tin, level the surface, then bake for 15 minutes until a toothpick inserted into the cake comes out clean. Leave in the tin to cool.

ORANGE JELLY LAYER
1 packet orange jelly (gelatine dessert) powder (enough to set 600ml/21fl oz water)
300ml (10½fl oz) almost boiling water
1 orange, cut into segments (no skin or pith)

1 Dissolve the jelly powder in the hot water.

2 Place the jelly in the fridge and check every 10 minutes to see if it is setting.

3 Once the jelly starts to set, pour it on top of the cake.

4 Add the orange segments, spaced evenly, and refrigerate until fully set.

CHOCOLATE MOUSSE LAYER
80g (2¾oz) dark chocolate (70% cocoa solids), chopped
80g (2¾oz) aquafaba (see Janusz Says on page 50)
2 tablespoons icing (confectioners') sugar, sifted

1 Heat the chocolate in the microwave on High in 15-second bursts, stirring after each burst, until melted. Leave the chocolate to cool but not set.

2 In a stand mixer with the whisk attachment, whisk the aquafaba until stiff peaks form – this will take much longer than egg whites. While whisking, gradually add the sugar, a teaspoon at a time, and mix until the sugar is fully incorporated and the mixture is no longer grainy.

3 Add the whipped aquafaba to the chocolate and fold it in using a spatula.

4 Pour the mousse on top of the set jelly layer.

5 Return to the fridge to set.

6 Remove the cake from the tin – (use a kitchen blowtorch to warm the sides of the tin to make it easier), and gently peel off the baking paper.

TO ASSEMBLE
1 tablespoon pure unsweetened cocoa powder, to dust

1 Dust the top of the cake with cocoa powder and serve.

2 Store in the fridge for up to 3 days.

With a chocolate biscuit base, creamy cheesecake filling and raspberry heart topping, here's a dessert that's sure to impress the one you love. Baked in a water bath for a smooth texture, this cheesecake is a labour of love that's definitely worth the effort.

'I LOVE YOU' CHEESECAKE

BISCUIT BASE

80g (2¾oz) chocolate biscuits filled with chocolate cream (e.g., Bourbon biscuits or chocolate-filled Oreos)
30g (1oz) unsalted butter, melted and cooled

CHEESECAKE

300g (10½oz) cream cheese, room temperature
75g (2½oz) sour cream
60g (2oz) caster (superfine) sugar
1 large egg, room temperature
1 teaspoon vanilla bean paste

RASPBERRY HEARTS

80g (2¾oz) raspberries
1 tablespoon caster (superfine) sugar
1 teaspoon cornflour (cornstarch)

1 Preheat the oven to 180°C (350°F). Line the base of a 15cm (6 inch) round springform cake tin with baking paper.

2 For the base, blitz the biscuits to a crumb in a food processor. Add the melted butter and mix until combined.

3 Press the biscuit base mixture into the bottom of the tin.

4 Bake for 10 minutes, then leave to cool in the tin.

5 For the cheesecake, whisk all the ingredients together until just combined – avoid overmixing.

6 For the raspberry hearts, combine the raspberries and sugar in a small saucepan over medium–high heat and cook until the raspberries begin to break apart.

7 Strain the raspberry mixture through a fine-mesh sieve into a bowl. Add the cornflour, mixing until combined and there are no lumps.

8 Pour the cheesecake mixture onto the biscuit base in the tin.

9 Use a teaspoon to place dots of the raspberry purée on top of the cheesecake mixture. Create a heart shape by dragging a toothpick through the raspberry purée dots to join them up.

10 Preheat the oven to 160°C (315°F).

11 Cover the base and side of the cheesecake tin with foil so no water will get in. Place the tin into a larger roasting tin.

12 Pour boiling water into the larger tin until it reaches halfway up the side of the cheesecake tin. Bake for 30 minutes. Switch off the oven but leave the cheesecake to cool inside for 1 hour.

13 Remove from the oven and chill the cheesecake in the fridge for at least 12 hours.

14 Store in the fridge for up to 4 days.

Serve your Pride party guests something quirky with this tray of sweet nachos. With cinnamon sugar-coated 'corn chips' drizzled in caramel sauce, and served with a sweetened vanilla cream, this snack with a twist is sure to get guests dancing to the mariachi.

SWEET NACHOS

CINNAMON CORN CHIPS

190g (6¾oz) plain (all-purpose) flour, sifted
2 egg yolks, room temperature
1 tablespoon dark rum
pinch of salt
75g (2½oz) sour cream
500ml (17fl oz) vegetable oil, for frying
50g (1¾oz) caster (superfine) sugar
1 tablespoon ground cinnamon

1   In a stand mixer with the dough hook attachment, mix the flour, egg yolks, rum, salt and sour cream until a stiff dough forms. Wrap the dough in plastic wrap and let it rest at room temperature for 30 minutes.

2   Transfer the dough to a floured work surface. Lightly bash it with the end of a rolling pin to flatten, gather it up and then bash again. Repeat this process for around 15 minutes; this incorporates air into the dough, making it nice and crispy when fried.

3   Roll the dough to 1–2mm (1⁄16 inch) thick. Using a pizza cutter, cut out corn chip-sized triangular shapes.

4   Heat the oil in a large, deep heavy-based frying pan, or deep-fryer, to 175°C (345°F).

5   Fry the chips in a couple of batches until golden brown on both sides, 1–2 minutes, turning them halfway through frying. When cooked, transfer the chips to a plate lined with paper towel to drain. Set aside to cool slightly.

6   Combine the caster sugar and cinnamon in a bowl.

7   Roll the cooked chips in the sugar and cinnamon mixture, then place in a serving dish.

CARAMEL SAUCE

150g (5½oz) caster (superfine) sugar
2 tablespoons water
1 tablespoon golden syrup (light corn syrup)
20g (¾oz) unsalted butter
80g (2¾oz) double (thick) cream
½ teaspoon vanilla bean paste

1   Combine the sugar, water and golden syrup in a small saucepan over medium–high heat. Cook, without stirring, until the temperature reaches 170°C (325°F) or until the sugar turns an amber colour.

2   Remove the pan from the heat and add the butter and cream – this will bubble up, so be careful! Mix the ingredients until combined.

3   Add the vanilla bean paste and mix until combined.

4   Return the pan to the heat and cook for 1 minute.

5   Remove the pan from the heat and allow to cool to room temperature.

WHIPPED VANILLA CREAM

200g (7oz) double (thick) cream
30g (1oz) icing (confectioners') sugar, sifted
1 teaspoon vanilla bean paste

1   In a stand mixer with the whisk attachment, whip all the ingredients until soft peaks form.

2   Transfer to a serving dish and refrigerate until ready to serve.

TO ASSEMBLE
20 fresh raspberries

1. Place the corn chips in a serving bowl. Spoon the cream over the chips and drizzle with some caramel sauce. Place the left-over caramel sauce in a small jug to serve alongside the nachos.

2. Top with raspberries and serve immediately.

3. The fried corn chips (by themselves) can be stored in an airtight container for up to 5 days.

MAKES 4 PAIRS OF GLASSES

Photo props are a must at any party, but how about ones you can eat? Inspired by Elton John, these chocolate biscuit frames can be piped into any shape to suit your party's theme and the coloured isomalt sugar lenses makes them even more extra. Iconic!

EDIBLE PARTY GLASSES

CHOCOLATE BISCUITS

125g (4½oz) unsalted butter, room temperature
75g (2½oz) icing (confectioners') sugar, sifted
½ teaspoon vanilla bean paste
1 large egg white, room temperature
150g (5½oz) plain (all-purpose) flour
15g (½oz) pure unsweetened cocoa powder
1 teaspoon cornflour (cornstarch)

1. Grease a baking tray and line it with baking paper – or use a silicone baking mat.

2. In a stand mixer with the paddle attachment, beat the butter until pale and creamy. While mixing, gradually add the sugar, a tablespoon at a time, until fully incorporated. While mixing, add the vanilla bean paste and egg white and mix until combined.

3. Sift the flour, cocoa powder and cornflour over the mixture and mix until a soft dough forms.

4. Transfer the dough to a piping bag with a 5mm (¼ inch) plain nozzle.

5. Pipe the dough into the shapes of decorative glasses such as squares, stars, hearts or cat eyes. You can use a real pair of sunglasses to draw around as a template for the shape of the lens and the position of the nose bridge.

6. Freeze the biscuits for 30 minutes.

7. Preheat the oven to 190°C (375°F).

8. Remove from the freezer and bake for 10 minutes. Leave to cool on the tray for 5 minutes, then transfer to a wire rack to cool completely.

PINK LENSES

100g (3½oz) clear isomalt
1 drop of pink gel food colouring

1. To make the lenses, melt the isomalt in the microwave on High for 1 minute, then stir and heat in 30-second bursts, stirring between each burst, until melted.

2. Remove from the microwave and add the food colouring, stirring until the mixture is an even colour.

3. Set the biscuits on a silicone mat or lined baking tray. Pour the isomalt into the eyeholes in the glasses. Do not touch them until they are cool.

DECORATIVE ICING (OPTIONAL)

1 large pasteurised egg white (pasteurised egg whites in cartons are sold at most supermarkets), room temperature
200g (7oz) icing (confectioners') sugar, sifted
1 teaspoon lemon juice
selection of gel food colourings

1. In a stand mixer with the whisk attachment, whisk the egg white until stiff peaks form. While whisking, gradually add the sugar, a tablespoon at a time, until fully incorporated and the mixture is no longer grainy. Add the lemon juice and mix to combine.

2. Divide the mixture evenly among separate bowls (depending on how many colours you are using). Add a different food colouring to each portion and mix until well combined and the colours are even.

TO ASSEMBLE

1   Transfer the different-coloured icings to small disposable piping bags with a small tip cut off each one.

2   If you like, you can decorate the glasses frames with bright bold colourful patterns that even Sir Elton would be impressed by!

3   Store the biscuits in an airtight container for up to 1 week.

Get ready to add some fun and colour to your baking with these delightful sprinkle-filled cupcakes, topped with raspberry jam and a swirl of vanilla cream frosting. They are perfect for a celebration or simply a sweet treat to brighten up any day.

FUNFETTI CUPCAKES

RAINBOW SPRINKLE CUPCAKES

80g (2¾oz) unsalted butter, room temperature
80g (2¾oz) caster (superfine) sugar
1 teaspoon vanilla bean paste
1 large egg, room temperature
1 egg yolk, room temperature
100g (3½oz) plain (all-purpose) flour
¾ teaspoon baking powder
2 tablespoons Greek-style yoghurt
20g (¾oz) rainbow sprinkles

VANILLA CREAM

300g (10½oz) double (thick) cream
100g (3½oz) mascarpone
40g (1½oz) icing (confectioners') sugar, sifted
1 teaspoon vanilla bean paste

TO ASSEMBLE

6 teaspoons raspberry jam
rainbow sprinkles

1. Preheat the oven to 180°C (350°F). Line six holes of a muffin tin with paper cases.

2. For the cupcakes, in a stand mixer with the paddle attachment, beat the butter until pale and creamy. While mixing, gradually add the sugar, a tablespoon at a time, until fully incorporated. Add the vanilla bean paste, egg and egg yolk and mix until combined.

3. Sift the flour and baking powder over the mixture and fold them in using a spatula.

4. Add the yoghurt and fold it in.

5. Add the sprinkles and fold them in.

6. Fill each paper case two-thirds full with batter and bake for 20 minutes until golden and a toothpick inserted into the cakes comes out clean. Leave to cool for a few minutes in the tin, then transfer to a wire rack to cool completely.

7. For the vanilla cream, in a stand mixer with the whisk attachment, whip the cream, mascarpone, sugar and vanilla bean paste until soft peaks form.

8. Transfer the mixture to a piping bag with a star nozzle.

9. Place the cupcakes on a serving plate. Top each cupcake with 1 teaspoon of jam.

10. Pipe vanilla cream in a swirl on top of the cupcakes, then scatter with the sprinkles.

11. Store in an airtight container in the fridge for up to 2 days.

One of my favourite experiences from childhood was helping my mother bake in the kitchen. I wanted to celebrate this by baking something in honour of every child's favourite part of baking – licking the bowl! This recipe makes butter 'tongue' biscuits that are used to scoop up generous helpings of safe-to-eat cake batter.

LICK-THE-BOWL CAKE BATTER & TONGUE BISCUITS

TONGUE BISCUITS
85g (3oz) unsalted butter, room temperature
85g (3oz) caster (superfine) sugar
2 large egg whites, room temperature
1 teaspoon vanilla bean paste
85g (3oz) plain (all-purpose) flour

CAKE BATTER
120g (4¼oz) plain (all-purpose) flour
90g (3¼oz) unsalted butter, room temperature
120g (4¼oz) soft light brown sugar
1 tablespoon double (thick) cream
1 teaspoon vanilla bean paste
25g (1oz) white chocolate chips
1 tablespoon full-cream (whole) milk
¼ teaspoon pink gel food colouring
25g (1oz) rainbow sprinkles

TO ASSEMBLE
10 fresh strawberries, quartered (with leaves on)

1 Preheat the oven to 180°C (350°F). Grease two baking trays and line them with baking paper.

2 For the biscuits, in a stand mixer with the paddle attachment, beat the butter until pale and creamy. While mixing, gradually add the sugar, a tablespoon at a time, until fully incorporated. Add the egg whites and vanilla bean paste and whisk to combine. Sift the flour over the mixture and fold it in using a spatula.

3 Transfer the mixture to a piping bag with an 8mm (⅜ inch) plain nozzle.

4 Pipe 8cm (3¼ inch) long biscuits onto the trays leaving large gaps between them as they will spread. (You will make about 25.)

5 Bake for 9–10 minutes until the edges are browned. Leave to cool on the trays.

6 For the cake batter, place the flour on a large plate and microwave on High for 30 seconds. Stir the flour, then return it to the microwave for a further 30 seconds. Repeat this process until the flour reaches 75°C (170°F) on a sugar thermometer.

7 In a stand mixer with the paddle attachment, beat the butter until pale and creamy. Add the sugar, a tablespoon at a time, and mix until the sugar is fully incorporated and the mixture is light and fluffy.

8 Sift the flour over the mixture and fold it in using a spatula.

9 Add the cream, vanilla bean paste, chocolate chips and milk and mix to combine using a spatula. Add the pink colouring to the bowl and mix until the colour is even.

10 Place the batter in a serving dish and mix the sprinkles through.

11 Serve the bowl of batter with the biscuits and fresh strawberries on the side for dipping.

12 The biscuits will keep for up to 4 days in an airtight container. The edible batter should be stored in an airtight container in the fridge and will keep for up to 4 days.

SERVES 8

Reader disclaimer: this cake contains mayonnaise! With the price of baking ingredients, I wanted to show that by using mayonnaise in place of eggs and oil, you save on cost but get just as much flavour. For those with an extra sweet tooth, the cake is decorated with Smarties – these are colourful candy-coated small round discs of chocolate, similar to M&Ms.

SMARTIES & MAYO CAKE

CHOCOLATE GANACHE
600g (1lb 5oz) double (thick) cream
250g (9oz) milk chocolate (35% cocoa solids), chopped
50g (1¾oz) dark chocolate (70% cocoa solids), chopped

1 Place the cream in a saucepan over medium–high heat and bring to the boil. Remove the pan from the heat. Add the milk and dark chocolate and leave to sit for 2 minutes, then stir until the chocolate is melted and the mixture is smooth.

2 Transfer to a large bowl and cover with plastic wrap touching the surface of the chocolate mixture, to prevent a skin forming.

3 Refrigerate for at least 12 hours.

MAYO CAKE
200g (7oz) whole-egg mayonnaise
200ml (7fl oz) buttermilk
160g (5½oz) caster (superfine) sugar
2 teaspoons instant espresso coffee granules
1 teaspoon vanilla bean paste
200g (7oz) plain (all-purpose) flour
1½ teaspoons bicarbonate of soda (baking soda)
75g (2½oz) pure unsweetened cocoa powder

1 Preheat the oven to 170°C (325°F). Grease three 15cm (6 inch) round springform cake tins and line the bases with baking paper.

2 In a stand mixer with the whisk attachment, whisk the mayonnaise, buttermilk, sugar, coffee and vanilla bean paste until combined. Sift the flour, bicarbonate of soda and cocoa over the mixture and mix until combined.

3 Divide the batter evenly among the cake tins, level the surfaces, then bake for 30 minutes until a toothpick inserted into the cakes comes out clean. Leave in the tins to cool completely, then remove from the tins.

TO ASSEMBLE
200g (7oz) fresh raspberries
300g (10½oz) rainbow Smarties or M&Ms

1 Remove the ganache from the fridge. In a stand mixer with the whisk attachment, whip the ganache until creamy – make sure not to overwhip it as it will become grainy.

2 Place one of the sponges on a cake board or serving plate. Cover with one-quarter of the ganache and top with half the raspberries. Place the second sponge on top and repeat the process. Place the third sponge on top and cover the top and side of the cake with ganache.

3 Transfer the left-over ganache to a piping bag with a star nozzle.

4 Separate your Smarties into colours. Decorate the side of the cake with double-width columns of one colour of the candy, to create a rainbow pattern.

5 Pipe blobs of ganache around the top of the cake, then top each blob with one Smartie. Fill the centre of the cake with the candy. Store in the fridge for up to 3 days but serve at room temperature.

SERVES 12

Got bundts, hun? You do now! When cut, this vanilla, rum and citrus-flavoured bundt cake reveals a stunning tie-dye rainbow sponge, topped with marbled icing and fragrant, edible flowers.

TIE-DYE RAINBOW BUNDT CAKE

BUNDT CAKE
3 large eggs, room temperature
200g (7oz) caster (superfine) sugar
210g (7½oz) plain (all-purpose) flour
1 teaspoon baking powder
150ml (5fl oz) full-cream (whole) milk
80g (2¾oz) unsalted butter
zest of 1 lemon
zest of 1 orange
1 tablespoon dark rum
1 tablespoon vanilla bean paste
2 drops each of red, orange, yellow, green, blue and purple gel food colouring

LEMON ICING
100g (3½oz) icing (confectioners') sugar, sifted
40ml (1¼fl oz) lemon juice, warm

TO ASSEMBLE
edible flowers

1 Preheat the oven to 180°C (350°F). Prepare a 23.5 x 9.5cm (9¼ x 3¾ inch) bundt tin by greasing it and dusting it with flour.

2 For the cake, in a stand mixer with the whisk attachment, whisk the eggs and sugar on high speed until light and fluffy.

3 Combine the flour and baking powder in a bowl.

4 Sift the dry ingredients over the wet mixture, folding it in using a spatula.

5 Combine the milk, butter, zests, rum and vanilla bean paste in a medium saucepan over high heat and bring to the boil.

6 Add this milk mixture to the flour mixture and gently fold in until just incorporated. Divide the batter evenly among six smaller bowls.

7 Add a different food colouring to each portion and gently mix through (but don't overmix; it's okay if the colour is not completely incorporated).

8 Transfer the coloured batters, a tablespoon at a time, into the bundt tin, alternating the colours as you go to create a tie-dye effect.

9 Bake for 45 minutes until a toothpick inserted into the cake comes out clean and the cake is a deep golden colour on top. Leave to cool in the tin for 5–10 minutes, then transfer to a wire rack to cool completely.

10 Prepare the icing by mixing the sugar with the warm lemon juice in a jug.

11 Pour the icing over the top of the cake, then top with edible flowers.

12 Store in an airtight container for up to 3 days.

This colourful, tasty, ombré carrot cake is a popular recipe of mine among friends and family thanks to a secret ingredient that makes it beautifully moist ... pineapple! But shhh ... don't tell anyone!

OMBRÉ CARROT CAKE

CARROT CAKE

425g (15oz) tinned pineapple slices in juice
3 large eggs, room temperature
125ml (4fl oz) vegetable oil
160g (5½oz) caster (superfine) sugar
2 tablespoons maple syrup
1 teaspoon vanilla bean paste
1 tablespoon orange zest
180g (6¼oz) plain (all-purpose) flour
1 teaspoon baking powder
1 teaspoon bicarbonate of soda (baking soda)
2 teaspoons ground cinnamon
½ teaspoon ground nutmeg
¼ teaspoon ground cloves
¼ teaspoon ground allspice
200g (7oz) grated carrots
150g (5½oz) chopped pecans

1 Preheat the oven to 180°C (350°F). Grease three 15cm (6 inch) round cake tins and line the bases with baking paper.

2 Drain the excess juice from the pineapple slices, then cut them into small pieces. Strain through a fine-mesh sieve placed over a bowl.

3 In a stand mixer with the whisk attachment, whisk the eggs, oil, sugar, maple syrup, vanilla bean paste and orange zest until combined.

4 Sift the flour, baking powder, bicarbonate of soda and spices over the mixture and mix to combine.

5 Add the grated carrot, pecans and pineapple and fold them in using a spatula.

6 Divide the batter evenly among the tins, level the surfaces, then bake for 30 minutes until a toothpick inserted into the cakes comes out clean.

7 Leave to cool in the tin for a few minutes, then transfer to a wire rack to cool completely.

CREAM CHEESE FROSTING

200g (7oz) unsalted butter, room temperature
400g (14oz) icing (confectioners') sugar, sifted
1 teaspoon vanilla bean paste
400g (14oz) cream cheese, room temperature

1 In a stand mixer with the paddle attachment, beat the butter until pale and creamy. While mixing, gradually add the sugar, a tablespoon at a time, until fully incorporated. Add the vanilla bean paste and mix to combine.

2 Reduce the speed to low and add the cream cheese. Mix just until combined as the longer you whip the more watery the frosting will become.

TO ASSEMBLE

1 drop each of red, orange, yellow, green, blue and purple gel food colouring

1 Place the first sponge on a cake board or serving plate and spread one-quarter of the frosting over the top.

2 Place the second sponge on top and cover with another one-quarter of the frosting.

3 Top with the third sponge, then cover the top and side of the cake with the remaining frosting – there should be a little left over to create the ombré effect.

4 Divide the left-over frosting evenly among six bowls. Add a different food colouring to each portion and mix until the colours are even.

5 Use a palette knife to take ⅛ teaspoon amounts of each different-coloured frosting and paste them onto random spots on the cake. Repeat until the coloured frostings are used up.

6 Smooth the surface of the cake using a cake scraper or palette knife. The patches of different colour will spread to create a beautifully random ombré effect all over.

7 Store in the fridge for up to 3 days.

JANUSZ SAYS

With this cake you can get creative by using ombré colours that celebrate different parts of the LGBTQ+ community and their individual flag colours.

MAKES 10

These treats are easy to make and reveal all the colours of the rainbow once bitten into. Whether you're hosting a Pride party or simply want to bake a fun treat for yourself, these Pride party balls are sure to bring plenty of joy.

PRIDE PARTY BALLS

250g (9oz) store-bought vanilla cake mix

120g (4½oz) cream cheese, room temperature

10 drops of natural custard flavouring (or your favourite flavouring)

3 drops each of red, orange, yellow, green, blue and purple gel food colouring

200g (7oz) white chocolate, chopped

30g (1oz) rainbow sprinkles

1   Spread the cake mix on a plate and heat in the microwave on High for 30 seconds. Stir and repeat the process three more times. Set aside to cool.

2   In a medium bowl using hand-held electric beaters, mix the cream cheese and custard flavouring until just combined – do not overwhip or the mixture will become watery. Add the cooled cake mix and mix until a firm dough forms.

3   Divide the dough into six equal portions and place each portion in a separate small bowl.

4   Add a different food colouring to each bowl. Mix until well combined and the colours are even.

5   Cover each bowl with plastic wrap and chill in the fridge for 1 hour.

6   Grease a baking tray and line it with baking paper.

7   Divide the red dough into 10 even pieces and lightly flatten them with your fingers. Place them on a sheet of baking paper, leaving gaps between them. Repeat the process with the remaining colours. If the dough gets too sticky, place it in the freezer for 10 minutes and it will be easier to work with.

8   Take a piece of each coloured dough and stack the pieces on top of each other in rainbow colour order – starting with red and finishing with purple.

9   Roll each stack of dough into a smooth ball and place them on the baking tray.

10 Chill in the fridge for 1 hour.

11 Grease a second baking tray and line it with baking paper.

12 Place the chocolate in a glass or metal bowl on top of a saucepan of simmering water, making sure the base of the bowl is not touching the water. Stir until the chocolate is melted.

13 Remove the dough balls from the fridge. Pick up one dough ball with a fork and submerge it completely into the melted chocolate. Lift the fork and tap it on the side of the bowl to remove any excess coating. Place the ball on the second tray and scatter sprinkles on top. Repeat with the remaining balls.

14 Allow the rainbow balls to set completely for 30 minutes before serving.

15 Store in an airtight container in the fridge for up to 3 days but serve at room temperature.

INDEX

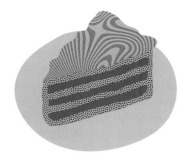

ACKNOWLEDGEMENTS

There are so many people I want to thank who have made this book possible, so I'll start from the beginning...

To the LGBTQ+ elders that came before me, thank you for fighting for change and creating a world where we can celebrate queer pride every day.

To my parents, Alicja and Jan Domagala, thank you for raising me without judgement and pushing me to pursue new adventures in life. We may be miles apart but you are with me every day.

To my sister Ula, brother-in-law Mariusz and my one-of-a-kind nieces and nephew, Gosia, Marysia and Julek, thank you for keeping me young and following your own dreams.

To Kasia, thank you for your true friendship over the years and for sharing countless bottles of wine (and one bottle of Limoncello).

To Eliza, Olga, Vicki, Lizzie, Katie, Jack, Simon, Dondon, Ren, Charlotte and Loz, thank you for being my friends and biggest cheerleaders.

To my British family, Nicki, Dan, Chloe, Phoebe, Billie, Ralph, George, Molly, Simon, Donna and Richard, thank you for making me a member of your weird and wonderful family and for your support, guidance and understanding always.

To Love Productions and their incredible team that became family, thank you for taking a chance on me and supporting me through the most exciting chapter of my life so far, and for making everything that's happened since possible.

To my fellow bakers, thank you for continuing to inspire me and becoming genuine friends and family for life: Maisam Algirgeet, James Dewar, Carole Edwards, Sandro Farmhouse, Kevin Flynn, Will Hawkins, Dawn Hollyoak, Rebs Lightbody, Maxy Maligisa, Abdul Rehman Sharif and Syabira Yusoff.

To Dawn Hollyoak: your strength, wit, kindness, passion for baking and generosity in sharing your incredible skills and tips (which are embedded throughout this book) are just a few of the things I love most about you. Thank you for being a mentor but most of all, my friend.

To Céline, Ariana, Kristy, Virginia and everyone involved at Murdoch Books, thank you for giving me this opportunity and allowing me to create a Pride-themed baking book I can be proud of.

To Keiron and Frankie, thank you for your artistry and for creating magic during a heatwave!

To Nigel, thank you for bringing equal levels of love, chaos and companionship to my life, and for the well-needed walkies in between writing and baking.

Lastly to Simon, I am extremely grateful for your support and love. Your encouragement and belief in me made this book possible. I cherish you more than words can express, and this journey wouldn't be possible without your constant presence and inspiration.

Published in 2024 by Murdoch Books, an imprint
of Allen & Unwin

Murdoch Books UK
Ormond House
26–27 Boswell Street
London WC1N 3JZ
Phone: +44 (0) 20 8785 5995
murdochbooks.co.uk
info@murdochbooks.co.uk

Murdoch Books Australia
Cammeraygal Country
83 Alexander Street
Crows Nest NSW 2065
Phone: +61 (0)2 8425 0100
murdochbooks.com.au
info@murdochbooks.com.au

For corporate orders and custom publishing,
contact our business development team at
salesenquiries@murdochbooks.com.au

Publisher: Céline Hughes
Editorial Manager: Virginia Birch
Design Manager: Kristy Allen
Designer: George Saad
Editor: Ariana Klepac
Photographer: Frankie Turner
Illustrator: George Saad
Prop Stylist: Agathe Gits
Food Stylist: Keiron George
Food Styling Assistant: Jess Ransom
Production Director: Lou Playfair

ISBN 978 1 92261 695 1

A catalogue record for this book is available from
the British Library

 A catalogue record for this
book is available from the
National Library of Australia

Colour reproduction by Splitting Image Colour Studio
Pty Ltd, Wantirna, Victoria
Printed by 1010 Printing International Limited, China

OVEN GUIDE: You may find cooking times vary
depending on the oven you are using. The recipes
in this book are based on fan-assisted oven
temperatures. For non-fan-assisted ovens, as a
general rule, set the oven temperature to 20°C (35°F)
higher than indicated in the recipe.

TABLESPOON MEASURES: We have used 20 ml
(4 teaspoon) tablespoon measures. If you are using a
15 ml (3 teaspoon) tablespoon add an extra teaspoon
of the ingredient for each tablespoon specified.

IMPORTANT: Those who might be at risk from the
effects of salmonella poisoning (the elderly, pregnant
women, young children and those suffering from
immune deficiency diseases) should consult their
doctor with any concerns about eating raw eggs.

10 9 8 7 6 5 4 3 2 1

FSC
www.fsc.org
MIX
Paper | Supporting
responsible forestry
FSC® C016973